# Nancy J. Cohen

## A Bad Hair Day
# COOKBOOK

Recipes from Nancy J. Cohen's
Cozy Mystery Series

A BAD HAIR DAY COOKBOOK, Copyright © 2019 by Nancy J. Cohen
Published by Orange Grove Press
Printed in the United States of America

Digital ISBN: 978-0-9997932-4-4
Print ISBN: 978-0-9997932-5-1
Cover Design by Boulevard Photografica
Digital Layout by www.formatting4U.com

This book includes a collection of recipes modified or created by the author. Any resemblance to another recipe is purely coincidental. These recipes are to be followed at the reader's own risk. It is the reader's responsibility to ensure that none of the ingredients are personally harmful to one's health. The author will not be held liable for any damage, medical or otherwise, resulting from the reader making these recipes.

The excerpts included in this book are works of fiction. Names, characters, places, and incidents either are the product of the author's imagination or are used fictitiously, and any resemblance to actual persons, business establishments, events or locales is entirely coincidental.

ORANGE
GROVE
PRESS

# Meet the Sleuth

Hairstylist Marla Vail is a salon owner with a nose for crime and a knack for exposing people's secrets. She lives in Palm Haven, Florida with her homicide detective husband, his teenage daughter, and their two dogs. When not busy working, she likes to cook, take walks in the park, meet her friends for lunch, go shopping, and solve murders. A caring person and a loyal friend, she fixes clients' hair with her expert styling skills and uses her sleuthing ability to pursue justice.

For more details and to join the Author's newsletter, please visit NancyJCohen.com

# Table of Contents

# Introduction
## by Marla Vail

Whether you're a skilled cook or an eager novice, this cookbook will have you in and out of the kitchen in no time. I am as busy as you are between juggling work at my hair salon with family obligations and solving crimes. So I tend to make recipes that aren't overly time-consuming.

But I've forgotten to introduce myself. I'm Marla Vail, hairstylist and salon owner. I live in sunny South Florida where it gets so hot in the summer that you could sizzle an egg on the sidewalk. Like you, I'm an on-the-go type person. This means I don't have a whole lot of time to slave over a stove. While I believe in making recipes from scratch, I'll often use a quick biscuit or cake mix when convenient. This is especially true for desserts. While I can bake, I'd rather put more time into cooking a meal than creating a fancy confection. You'll find both types of recipes in these pages.

My mother acted as a role model for me in the cooking arena. She served our family a hot meal every day. Her rules were strict. My brother Michael and I were not permitted to watch television during dinner, and we had to sit at the table until everyone was done. We divided up the cleaning chores. I'll probably do the same when my husband, Detective Dalton Vail, and I have children.

Food always brings families together, whether it's for daily meals or for celebrations. My Dad always said the extended family got together when you're bred, when you're wed, and when you're dead. He might be right, but let's not wait that long to make an impression in the kitchen.

If you're hesitant to start, wait for a Bad Hair Day, when nasty weather is getting you down and causing your hair to frizz. Ma always told me if I got depressed, the way out of it was to plan a dinner party. Whip out your whisk, snatch up your spoon, and prepare your palate. Inside the pages of this book are recipes that will bring you good cheer. You can make a dish for two or try a recipe for a houseful of guests. Either way, the directions are easy to follow.

Don't be afraid to be creative and add your own embellishments. The key is to be organized. Gather the ingredients before you assemble a dish. That way you won't be running back and forth between the pantry, the refrigerator, and the sink. You'll have everything you need right at your fingertips.

If you're looking for pork or ham recipes, you won't find them in these pages. I grew up in a kosher home, and even though I don't follow the practice in my own kitchen, I still feel reluctant to have these foods in my house. I can't say the same for shrimp, however. I know what you're thinking, but that's the way it is.

I can't end this chat without giving a nod of thanks to my author, Nancy J. Cohen. She was invaluable in helping me write this cookbook. While she makes no claims to be a professional baker or chef, she enjoys cooking for family and friends. You can find select photos of the dishes included here on her Facebook Page.

Reader feedback is really important to us. Please keep in touch through Nancy's newsletter at https://nancyjcohen.com /newsletter or contact her at nancy@nancyjcohen.com to tell her how you liked these recipes or to suggest ideas for the next edition. Happy Cooking!

# Cooking Tips

Gather all your ingredients before you assemble a dish. This will save you steps and time. If a recipe calls for oven baking/roasting, preheat the oven at the start. Temperatures given are in degrees Farenheit.

Buy bunches of fresh parsley and dill. Remove stems, rinse in colander, squeeze dry, and separate into plastic sandwich bags at a handful each. Squeeze air out and seal. Put in the freezer for later use in dishes that call for these herbs.

If you're one of the few people who doesn't like cilantro, blame it on your genes. You have an extra olfactory gene that allows you to detect the smell of aldehyde chemicals, found in both cilantro and soap. So to you, cilantro has an unpleasant taste. You can avoid the issue by using parsley instead of cilantro in your recipes.

For fresh produce, including herbs such as basil and rosemary, trim off the woody stems and tough stalks before using in a recipe. Rosemary can be cut into sprigs and chopped. Or you can remove the needle-like leaves by sliding your fingers down the stems.

When bananas become overripe, you can peel and freeze them. Thaw slightly to use later in recipes like Banana Bran Muffins or Banana Chocolate Chip Loaf.

Many of my recipes skip the addition of extra salt. If this isn't a concern for you, add salt at will. Try to use a variety, like kosher salt, without added iodide for cooking purposes. I also buy low or reduced sodium products when available. This is a personal choice and may not apply to you. But it's always good if you can substitute other flavorful herbs for salt when possible.

Instead of garlic powder, you could substitute granulated garlic. It has a milder flavor and less tendency to clump in wet recipes. The grind is a bit coarser than garlic powder. Both may contain additives to prevent caking.

Fresh ginger can be peeled and stored, covered by vodka, in a small jar in the refrigerator for several weeks. When ready to use, cut off the amount you need, pat it dry with a paper towel, and grate, slice or dice it for your recipe.

I use the term powdered sugar in my dessert recipes. This means confectioners 10x sugar as found in the grocery store. This finely ground sugar contains cornstarch to prevent caking. The 10x designation refers to the number of times the sugar has been processed to produce a fine powder.

Serving sizes given are guess-timates. For example, let's say you have a meal with 8 pieces of chicken thighs. I might say it serves 4 to 6. This depends on the appetites of your eaters. I'll eat only one piece, but my husband might eat two or more. Ditto for chicken breasts. I cut one in half for my portion but my husband will eat the whole thing. Regarding casseroles, eaters might only take a spoonful, or they might want second helpings. So view the serving sizes as a guideline and not an absolute measurement.

For soups, stews, and casseroles, feel free to add any fresh vegetables you have at home or substitute your favorites for some of the ingredients listed.

When using eggplant in a recipe, my preference is to peel the skin. You can eat the skin as it contains antioxidants, but it's tough to chew when thick. Also, you should salt the slices and let them sit for a half hour, then rinse and pat dry with a paper towel. This gets rid of any bitter juices from the seeds. As for the flesh, eggplant contains chlorogenic acid, which supposedly has anti-cancer properties. Always buy an eggplant that is firm to the touch.

Flour used in these recipes means all-purpose unbleached white flour. This is my personal choice. You can use bleached flour as it's a bit softer and may make fluffier desserts.

Regarding the use of cornstarch or flour as a thickening agent, cornstarch can be added last-minute, but flour needs to be cooked to lose its doughy flavor. Flour comes from wheat and contains protein as well as small amounts of fat. Cornstarch derives purely from corn and has no distinctive taste. Flour gives a lighter or more opaque result while sauces with cornstarch come out clear. Their ratios with water are different, too, so be sure to follow instructions on a recipe. You'll use about half the amount of cornstarch as flour. Be careful not to overcook the cornstarch, or the gel may break down. Note that cornstarch doesn't freeze as well as flour in recipes.

If you want to cook an ear of corn without boiling or grilling, stick the entire corn with the husk in the microwave. Cook it on high for 4 minutes. Remove the corn (use oven mittens as it will be hot) and place it on a cutting board. Slice off both ends. The husk will peel right off. If you wish to scrape the kernels, position the ear of corn over the hole in a tube pan and scrape down the sides.

# APPETIZERS

# ARTICHOKE DIP

*My friend, Tally, served this at one of her dinner parties. She said it was simple to make so I asked for the recipe. It's an easy-to-prepare appetizer that is handy to make last-minute if you keep the ingredients in stock. The hot dish gives a nice presentation for guests and a tempting aroma to scent your kitchen.*

## Ingredients

14 oz. can artichoke hearts, drained and chopped
1 cup light mayonnaise
1 cup grated Parmesan cheese
Garlic powder
Paprika

## Directions

Preheat oven to 350 degrees. In a medium bowl, mix the chopped artichokes, mayonnaise, and Parmesan cheese. Add garlic powder to taste. Pour mixture into small baking dish and sprinkle paprika on top. Bake for 20 to 30 minutes or until bubbly. Serve with crackers.

Nancy J. Cohen

# ASPARAGUS CHEESE POCKETS

*My stepdaughter, Brianna, experimented with this recipe. It requires a few steps but the effort is worth the impressive results. Serve on a platter or on individual plates as a starter course for a sit-down meal.*

## Ingredients

$1/_2$ pound fresh asparagus, trimmed
4 oz. cream cheese, softened
1 Tbsp. low fat milk
2 Tbsp. mayonnaise
1 Tbsp. chopped onion
1 Tbsp. diced pimento, drained
8 oz. tube refrigerated crescent rolls
Cooking spray

## Directions

Preheat oven to 375 degrees. Microwave asparagus with 2 Tbsp. water in a covered microwave-safe container for 2 minutes. Let stand, covered, for 1 more minute. Cut asparagus into one-inch pieces and set aside. In a medium bowl, beat together the cream cheese, milk, and mayonnaise. Stir in onions and pimento.

Unroll the crescent dough into eight separate triangles. Place on an ungreased baking sheet. Spread 1 Tbsp. cream cheese mixture onto each triangle. Add asparagus pieces on top. Fold corners of dough together to hold filling inside. Lightly coat the pockets with cooking spray. Bake until browned, about 12 to 15 minutes. Serves 8.

# BAKED EGG ROLLS

*This is a healthy alternative to buying store-bought fried egg rolls. Make them for a party or serve them as the first course at an Asian-themed dinner. I may not be as fond of sushi as my friends, but I do like spring rolls and steamed dumplings when I dine out. These are a good homemade option for an afternoon snack as well as a party appetizer.*

## Ingredients

1 pound frozen broccoli stir-fry vegetable blend, thawed
1 cup shredded cooked chicken
4½ tsp. low sodium soy sauce
2 tsp. sesame oil
2 garlic cloves, minced
½ tsp. ground ginger
8 oz. all-purpose pasta or egg roll wrappers
1 egg, beaten
1 jar of duck sauce

## Directions

Preheat oven to 400 degrees. In a bowl, combine ½ package chopped, defrosted vegetables, chicken, soy sauce, sesame oil and spices. Place ¼ cup mixture into the center of each wrapper. Fold bottom corner over filling then fold two sides toward the center. Moisten flap of remaining corner with beaten egg and seal.

Place egg rolls seam side down on a greased baking sheet. Spray tops of wrappers with nonstick cooking spray or brush with beaten egg. Bake for 15 minutes or until browned. Makes 8 servings. Recipe may be doubled. Serve warm with duck sauce.

# CHILI DIP

*This is another hot, bubbly dish to serve as an appetizer. It goes well with a Mexican-themed dinner party.*

## Ingredients

15 oz. jar Cheese Whiz
15 oz. can Hormel chili without beans
1 bunch green onions, chopped
4 oz. can diced green chilies
$1/4$ tsp. tabasco sauce

## Directions

Preheat oven to 275 degrees. Mix all ingredients and bake for 45 minutes or until bubbly. Serve with large corn chips.

# CROISSANT BRIE APPETIZERS

*These yummy melted cheese bites will have you smacking your lips and asking for more. If you're not a fan of brie, use shredded mozzarella or Swiss instead, or whatever cheese you have on hand. The same goes for the jam. You can substitute your favorite variety for the strawberry.*

## Ingredients

4 fresh croissants
8 oz. brie cheese
8 Tbsp. chopped walnuts
8 Tbsp. strawberry jam

## Directions

Cut croissants in half lengthwise. Lay a quarter of an inch slice of brie on each cut side of croissant and sprinkle with 1 Tbsp. chopped walnuts. Melt in microwave for 30 seconds. Spread 1 Tbsp. jam for each half on top of melted cheese. Cut halves into quarters and serve warm. Makes 8 servings.

# EGGPLANT DIP

*My mom inherited this recipe from her mother. I remember visiting Grandma's house. She had one of those wooden bowls with a hand-held chopper that she used in the days before food processors. I kept those items as a remembrance of her and have them stashed in my pantry. At least if there's a power outage, I'll have a way to chop my vegetables. Grandma would bake the eggplant on top of her gas range on a device that was flat on the bottom with a domed top. It would take about an hour for the eggplant to soften. How lucky we are to have microwaves and processors. If you have leftovers from this dish after a party, make a sandwich with some eggplant dip, lettuce, and tomato slices.*

## Ingredients

1 large, firm eggplant
$^1/_2$ large sweet onion, peeled
1 Tbsp. olive oil
Salt to taste
Crackers

## Directions

Rinse eggplant and place on cutting board. Puncture one side in two or three places with fork. Place eggplant in microwave with punctured side up. Cook on high until soft and pliant, in 5-minute increments, for about 15 minutes.

Let the eggplant cool on cutting board, then slice in half length-wise without cutting all the way through. Open eggplant halves and scoop out the pulp into a bowl. Discard the peel. In a food processor, chop onion. Add eggplant and puree with onions. Stir in olive oil and salt to taste. Serve as a dip with crackers.

# GUACAMOLE

*Dalton and I went into a Señor Frog's on our Caribbean Cruise and ordered this dish. The waiter rolled a cart to our table and made it fresh while we watched. It was the best guacamole I'd ever had. I made a note of the ingredients, and this is the closest I can come to emulating that recipe. Regarding the onions, use whichever type appeals to you. Red onions would work fine if you prefer them over white onions. If you're a cilantro fan, you can substitute this herb for the parsley. Be creative and use ingredients that suit your taste.*

## Ingredients

2 ripe avocados
8 oz. container fresh diced tomatoes, drained
8 oz. container chopped fresh onions
1 Tbsp. chopped fresh parsley
Juice from 1 fresh lime
Salt to taste
Tortilla Chips

## Directions

Mix together chopped tomatoes, onions, and the scooped-out insides of two ripe avocados. Stir in parsley and lime juice. Add salt to taste. Pour into a serving bowl and serve with tortilla chips.

# HAROSET

*This recipe appears in* Highlights to Heaven *during a Passover scene. It's served as part of the Seder meal and represents the mortar the Hebrew slaves used to build bricks for the Pharaoh of Egypt. I usually indulge in more than one spoonful at the meal as I like this once-a-year treat. You can also serve it to company as an appetizer with crackers.*

## Ingredients

$1/_2$ cup ground walnuts
2 apples, peeled, cored, and chopped
3 Tbsp. sweet kosher wine
$1/_2$ tsp. cinnamon
1 Tbsp. honey

## Directions

Mix together all ingredients and put into a serving bowl. Serve with matzo crackers.

# HOT DOG CRESCENTS

*My Dad had a fondness for hot dogs, so my mother found this recipe to please him as a party appetizer. He always hoped for leftovers so he could reheat these crescents for lunch the next day.*

## Ingredients

8 beef hot dogs
8 oz. sharp cheddar cheese
8 oz. tube refrigerated crescent rolls

## Directions

Preheat oven to 375 degrees. Slit hot dogs lengthwise to within $^1/_2$ inch of ends. Cut block of cheese into one-quarter-inch slices. Cut these lengthwise to get 2 x ½ inch strips. Insert cheese into hot dog slits. Separate crescent rolls into triangles. Place hot dog on shortest side of each triangle and roll up. Put crescents cheese-side up on greased baking sheet. Bake for 12 to 15 minutes or until golden brown. Serve as appetizer or as lunch with chips on the side. Serves 8.

# PORTOBELLO MUSHROOM APPETIZER

*I had this at a friend's house and liked it so much that I asked for the recipe. I'll make a meal of it along with a salad, or serve it as a starter course for a dinner party.*

## Ingredients

4 large Portobello mushrooms, stemmed and cleaned
4 Tbsp. balsamic vinegar
1 large ripe tomato, sliced
4 oz. shredded mozzarella cheese
0.75 oz. package fresh basil, trimmed and chopped
Olive oil

## Directions

Preheat oven to 350 degrees. Scrape gills out of underside of mushrooms. Rinse and pat dry with paper towels. Place mushrooms top side down on greased baking sheet. In each mushroom hollow, sprinkle 1 Tbsp. balsamic vinegar. Top with tomato slice, mozzarella cheese, fresh basil, and a few sprinkles of olive oil. Bake for 15 minutes. Serves 4.

# SPINACH ARTICHOKE DIP

*This is similar to the artichoke dip above but with added spinach. If I'm in a rush, I'll buy the store-bought version, but I always prefer to control the ingredients when I have time to make a dish from scratch.*

## Ingredients

14 oz. can artichoke hearts, drained and chopped
10 oz. package frozen chopped spinach, thawed and drained
$3/4$ cup Parmesan cheese
$3/4$ cup light mayonnaise
$1/2$ cup reduced fat shredded mozzarella cheese
$1/2$ tsp. garlic powder

## Directions

Preheat oven to 350 degrees. Mix all ingredients. Spoon into greased baking dish. Bake for 20 minutes or until heated through. Serve with crackers.

# SPINACH BALLS

*My cousin, Cynthia, hosts the Taste of the World charity fundraiser each holiday season to benefit her favorite ocean preservation society. One of the chefs made these simple but tasty little spinach balls one year. I just had to get the recipe. Cynthia knows I like them, so she makes these for an appetizer whenever she hosts Thanksgiving for the family.*

## Ingredients

(2) 10 oz. packages frozen chopped spinach, thawed and squeezed dry
2 cups crushed herb stuffing mix
1 cup grated Parmesan cheese
$1/_2$ cup melted butter
4 green onions, chopped
3 eggs, beaten

## Directions

Preheat oven to 350 degrees. Combine ingredients in a large bowl and mix well. Shape into 1-inch balls. Cover and refrigerate or freeze until ready to bake. Bake on an ungreased baking sheet for 10 to 15 minutes or until golden brown. Serve with your favorite mustard.

# SPINACH PUMPERNICKEL DIP

*This one is a favorite party dish of my mother's. She makes the hollowed center into a perfect circle, a feat I never seem able to accomplish. When I make it, Dalton eats half the bread pieces before I can put the plate out. You can save any leftover spinach dip and use it for the stuffed mushrooms below. If you make enough to start, this dip can serve double duty.*

## Ingredients

10 oz. package frozen chopped spinach, thawed and squeezed dry
1 package dry onion soup mix
$1^1/_2$ cups sour cream
1 cup mayonnaise
8 oz. can sliced water chestnuts, drained and chopped
3 green onions, chopped
1 round pumpernickel bread

## Directions

Mix together soup mix, sour cream, and mayonnaise until blended. Add spinach, water chestnuts, and green onions. Cover and chill. Just before serving, cut circle into top of bread and hollow out a bowl shape, saving pieces of bread to place around platter for dip. Spoon spinach mixture into hollow and serve.

# STUFFED MUSHROOMS

*I have to admit I'll cheat if I am in a hurry and substitute store-bought spinach artichoke dip or flavored cream cheese for the stuffing. Whichever way you make it, your mushrooms will be a hit. Leftovers are great the next morning with scrambled eggs. If you have any extra mixture, use it for a spinach dip.*

## Ingredients

(2) 16 oz. packages whole white mushrooms
3 oz. package cream cheese, softened
$1/2$ cup mayonnaise
$1/2$ cup sour cream
14 oz. can artichoke hearts, drained and chopped
10 oz. package frozen chopped spinach, thawed and squeezed dry
$1/3$ cup shredded mozzarella cheese
$3/4$ tsp. garlic powder
4 Tbsp. shredded Parmesan cheese
2 Tbsp. grated Parmesan cheese

## Directions

Preheat oven to 400 degrees. Remove stems from mushrooms and discard or save for another use. Clean mushrooms and pat dry with paper towel. Meanwhile, beat cream cheese, mayonnaise, and sour cream in a small bowl. Add artichokes, spinach, mozzarella cheese, garlic powder, and shredded Parmesan cheese.

Fill each mushroom cap with 1 Tbsp. spinach mixture. Place mushrooms on greased baking sheet and sprinkle with grated Parmesan cheese. Bake for 20 minutes or until tender. Transfer to platter and serve warm.

## HIGHLIGHTS TO HEAVEN
### Bad Hair Day Mystery #5

**The Recipes**
Haroset

*This is normally served as part of the Passover Seder, but you can also prepare it as an appetizer with crackers.*

**The Story**

Hairstylist and amateur sleuth Marla Shore lands a case close to home when her animal-loving neighbor—a man aptly named Goat—disappears, leaving his pets alone and a dead body in his master bedroom. Even more disturbing is the pattern of highlights Marla notes in the victim's hair. She recognizes the signature technique of her former mentor, master stylist Cutter Corrigan. Soon she's untangling clues that link Goat, Cutter, and the unsavory pet fur trade to her own past. Someone at her former beauty school has a hair-raising secret worth killing to keep.

**Passover Seder Excerpt**

Once people had settled, Arnie opened his Haggadah. "We'll begin on page nine. Since this is Jill's first Passover celebration, I'll explain things as we go along. Here is the Seder plate." As tradition warranted, he held up each item as he spoke about it. "The roasted bone stands for the lamb our ancestors sacrificed for the holiday. This roasted egg reminds us of the destruction of the holy temple. These bitter herbs stand for the bitter life our ancestors suffered as slaves in Egypt. And the Haroset represents the mortar they used to build bricks for the Pharaoh."

Marla remembered she had to make the Haroset for tomorrow night's Seder. Thankfully, it was an easy dish, and she

15

had in stock the chopped walnuts, apples, cinnamon, and kosher wine. She watched dutifully as Arnie explained about the Karpas, holding up a sprig of parsley, symbol of regrowth. Matzo, the bread of affliction, came next, in its three-tiered cloth holder.

Then the blessings began. Jill lit the candles, and Arnie said Kiddush before everyone drank the first of four cups of wine for the evening. The children giggled, this being the one time they were allowed to sip a sample from the grown-ups' glasses, although their own glasses held grape juice.

Marla's stomach rumbled with hunger as Arnie alternated between Hebrew and English in reading how their ancestors were delivered from bondage in Egypt. It was an ageless story celebrating freedom and decrying the oppression of people everywhere. They sang "Go Down Moses" and "Dayenu" and dipped their little fingers into wine for each of the ten plagues brought upon the Pharaoh. Marla visualized the movie version with Charlton Heston as Moses. Ma had made her and Michael watch *The Ten Commandments* every year. She'd never admit to anyone it was one of her favorite films.

These traditions were important to her, she realized. She could no more give them up than sacrifice her other rituals. Her thoughts drifted to Dalton, who clung to the past with similar tenacity. Perhaps his focus differed from hers, but this might be a common ground from which the well of a lasting relationship might spring.

Sustenance tonight came not from her epiphany but from the main meal following the second cup of wine. Marla dipped her piece of boiled potato into salt water, representing the tears of oppression. She ate her hardboiled egg, appreciating how it stood for eternal life. Everything had a meaning, but soon she became more interested in the food than the symbolism.

She chased down the starter course of gefilte fish with a bowl of matzo ball soup. By the time she got to the turkey and brisket, she was almost full and barely had room to scarf down a macaroon for dessert. No wonder their ancestors ate in a reclining position. They were stuffed!

After dinner, the kids opened the door to welcome Elijah the prophet. She used to believe his spirit actually drank from the full cup of wine on the table. *If he visited every Jewish household, he'd be mighty drunk by the night's end. Sort of like me.* She felt tipsy after singing more songs and downing more wine.

Forcing herself to remain sober, she accosted Jill as they carried dirty dishes into the kitchen. "I meant to ask you about Yani Verkovich's colleague," she said, admiring the glossy sheen of her friend's hair. "Did you identify him to Detective Vail?"

"The man's name is Lujan Chang." Jill put a couple of delicate crystal goblets near the sink.

"Did Chang mention what Yani was doing with Cutter?"

"I couldn't ask him direct questions, or he'd become suspicious. I pretended I was interviewing him as part of my public relations job. I told him I was looking for employees with interesting hobbies that we could use to improve our corporate image."

Marla grabbed a dish towel while Jill washed the crystal by hand. "Did he mention he collects birds, or anything about a connection to Wake Hollander, the pet-store owner?"

Jill gazed at her from under her long lashes. "Tell me about them again."

"Presumably Evan Fargutt imports birds or breeds them on his ranch. Evan sells them to Chang through Hollander. The man's obsession with birds does not explain why he goes to the local pound and collects dogs and cats destined for death row."

"He did ask me if I wanted to buy a fur coat for a cheap price."

"Maybe Chang was responsible for the skinned dog I found in Goat's backyard. Goat could have found out what he was doing and tried to save the animals."

"I thought you said Goat worked part-time on Evan's

ranch. How would he meet Chang, unless they'd run into each other on the property?"

Marla gripped the dish towel, excitement coursing through her. "It's possible they met at the pet store. Goat bought his supplies there."

"Yani may not have known about Chang's side business," Jill suggested. "Maybe Goat clued him in, and Yani got upset. Chang killed Yani to keep him quiet. He meant to silence Goat as well, but your neighbor got away."

"So what was Yani doing at Goat's house, and who brought the cash? Was Chang a passenger in the Corolla, or was he the motorcycle driver my other neighbor heard?"

Jill's brow furrowed. "Chang seemed glad Yani wasn't his lab partner anymore. Yani's sexual preferences bothered him. He didn't mention Cutter by name, but he said Yani had been bamboozled by a friend into believing he could perform miracles."

**ORDER NOW** at
https://nancyjcohen.com/highlights-to-heaven/

# BEVERAGES

# CITRUS CIDER

*This drink is welcome on a cold winter day. Treat yourself to a warm beverage or offer it to guests as a welcome drink at Thanksgiving dinner.*

## Ingredients

64 oz. bottle apple cider
$1/4$ cup brown sugar
$1/4$ cup thawed orange juice concentrate
3 cinnamon sticks
1 tsp. whole cloves
$1/4$ tsp. vanilla extract
Light rum (optional)

## Directions

In a large saucepan, combine apple cider, brown sugar, and orange juice concentrate. Tie cloves and cinnamon sticks into a cheesecloth bundle. Add the spice bundle to the cider mixture. Cover and simmer for 1 hour.

Remove spice packet from pot and stir in vanilla. Pour into individual glasses or mugs. If desired, add rum to taste. Serve warm or cold. Serves 6 to 8.

# FRUIT PUNCH

*My favorite drink on a Caribbean cruise is a rum punch. I'll order it when sitting on a beach in the islands, where waiters roam the sand taking orders. Have a few of these with enough rum, and you won't want to get up from your lounge chair. Somehow the mixed drinks on shore always seem to have more of a wallop than the ones on board the ship, so be careful.*

*I should have heeded my own advice in St. Maarten when I sampled the guavaberry liqueur. That one packed a punch, all right. I ended up passed out before I could reach the door. When I woke, I was locked in a strange house and in danger of missing the ship sailing... plus a lot more. You can read about this frightening episode in* Killer Knots.

## Ingredients

46 oz. can pineapple juice
12 oz. can frozen orange juice concentrate, thawed
2 liter bottle lemon-lime soda
Dash of Grenadine
Rum to taste

## Directions

Mix all ingredients in a large punch bowl. Ladle into individual cups over ice and serve.

# LIME PUNCH

*This colorful green beverage is great for a crowd. It's a refreshing cooler for a summer party. You can substitute Champagne or Prosecco for some of the soda if you wish, or add rum for a tropical libation.*

## Ingredients

2 quarts lime sherbet
2 liters lemon-lime soda
46 oz. can pineapple juice
32 oz. bottle cranberry juice
2 lemons, thinly sliced
3 limes, thinly sliced
10 oz. jar Maraschino cherries

## Directions

Spoon sherbet into a large punch bowl. Add 2 liters soda, one-half can of pineapple juice, and one-half jar of cranberry juice. Garnish with sliced lemons and limes. Add cherries, reserving enough to garnish each cup if desired. Ladle into individual cups and serve while still cold or over ice.

# PERMED TO DEATH

## Bad Hair Day Mystery #1

*Permed to Death doesn't contain recipes, but it features a poisoned cup of coffee. Because Marla gave the victim—a client at her salon—a cup of coffee right before the lady's demise, she becomes the prime suspect in a murder case. Marla meets Detective Dalton Vail for the first time in this debut title.*

### The Story

Sassy salon owner Marla Shore is giving grumpy Mrs. Kravitz a perm when her client dies in the shampoo chair. If that isn't enough to give her a bad hair day, handsome Detective Vail suspects Marla of poisoning the woman's coffee creamer. Figuring she'd better expose the real killer before the next victim frizzes out, Marla sets on the trail of a wave of wacky suspects. Her theory regarding whodunit gels only after she looks for the culprit closer to home.

### Excerpt from Permed to Death

"Marla, if the coffee is ready, I'll have a cup while my perm processes," Mrs. Kravitz said, squinting as Marla squeezed the pungent solution onto her scalp. "Be careful! I feel it dripping down my neck."

"I'll be done in a minute." Marla gritted her teeth as she bumped her hip against the shampoo sink. Already this promised to be an aggravating day. She'd had to come in early to accommodate Mrs. Kravitz, and the rest of her morning was fully booked. Not that Bertha Kravitz cared; she never considered anyone's needs except her own.

With efficiency born from years of practice, she wrapped Mrs. Kravitz's rods in a plastic cap, then set the timer for twenty minutes. After washing her hands, she poured her client a cup of coffee and added a package of sugar.

"Don't forget my powdered creamer," Mrs. Kravitz called.

"I've got it." Marla mixed in two spoonfuls from a reserved jar, frowning when her spoon scraped bottom. She hadn't realized the supply had dwindled so low. Sparing a moment to rinse the container at a sink, she tossed it into the trash while making a mental note to buy more later.

"Here you go." She handed Mrs. Kravitz the steaming mug.

"Marla, was that my jar you just discarded? I hope you have another one in stock because I'll want more coffee." Taking a sip, the woman winced. "Ugh, this tastes like medicine. How long has it been standing?"

"I just brewed a fresh pot before you came."

"Give me another package of sugar." While Marla complied, Mrs. Kravitz scanned the room like a vulture searching for prey. "Where are the bagels? I could use something to eat."

"I haven't had a chance to get them yet. Why don't you relax? You have less than fifteen minutes left on your timer. I'm going into the storeroom for some clean towels."

Scowling, Mrs. Kravitz took another sip of coffee.

Hoping to escape before the woman issued a new command, Marla rushed into the storage area. Her gaze scanned the shelves of chemicals, alighting on the neutralizer solution she'd selected earlier. She plucked it off its perch and was reaching for a pile of towels when a strangled sound struck her ears. A loud crash followed, like glass shattering.

Sprinting into the salon, Marla stared at Mrs. Kravitz, who slumped in the shampoo chair. Her bagged head lolled against the sink. The plastic cap wrapped around her rods had become dislodged, partially shading her face. Marla's gaze dropped to the floor where broken shards of the ceramic mug lay scattered amid a trail of dark liquid.

"Mrs. Kravitz?" she said, her heart thumping.

When there was no response, Marla stepped closer. Her client's face was distorted into a grimace. The woman's wide-set eyes, pupils dilated, stared blankly at the ceiling. She didn't appear to be breathing, unless her respirations were too shallow to notice.

"Mrs. Kravitz?" Marla repeated, her voice hoarse. Maybe the lady had fainted or been overwhelmed by fumes from the perm solution. Or else she'd fallen asleep. But then her chest would be moving, wouldn't it? And her eyes wouldn't be as vacant as—*Oh, God.*

Bile rising in her throat, Marla prodded the woman's arm, then jumped back when Mrs. Kravitz's hand flopped over the side of the chair, dangling like a cold, dead fish. A surge of nausea seized her as images from the past clouded her mind.

*You can't freeze up now, girl. Call for help.*

She rushed to the phone and dialed 911.

"Police, fire, or medical?" replied the dispatcher.

"Medical. I'm Marla Shore at the Cut 'N Dye Salon. One of my clients has stopped breathing. I think she's dead." Her voice cracking, she gave her street address.

"I'm notifying the rescue unit. They'll be there soon."

Marla replaced the receiver in its cradle, her hand trembling as a sense of déjà vu washed over her. Stiff with fear, she stood immobilized as memories from another time, another place, haunted her thoughts. A child's limp form, cradled in her arms. Her screams, echoing through a summer afternoon. Accusations, harsh and unforgiving. She hadn't known what to do then. Maybe she could make a difference now.

She dashed over to check the body for a pulse, forcing herself to feel the clammy wrist. Nothing. A faint odor, vaguely familiar, assailed her nostrils. Briefly, she wondered about performing CPR, but logic told her it was too late.

Sirens sounded outside, accompanied by the noise of screeching brakes. Any decision became unnecessary as a team of paramedics thundered in the front door. She stood aside while they performed their assessment.

A police officer arrived on the scene. After conferring with the medics, he asked Marla some preliminary questions. Numb with shock, she leaned against a counter while he notified his sergeant via cell phone. He mentioned something about a crime unit, so when several techs and a detective walked in, she wasn't surprised. Still, she wondered why they'd been called. Surely Mrs. Kravitz had a heart attack or a stroke.

Ignoring the technicians who scoured the salon, she focused on the steely-eyed detective approaching her. She could tell he was used to being in command from his set of wide shoulders, his determined stride, and the hawk-like expression on his angular face. Bushy eyebrows rose above a nose that might have been rearranged in his youth, indicating he wasn't averse to physical action when required. Faced with such a formidable symbol of authority, she quaked when he stopped in front of her.

Nervous, she began babbling. "I didn't realize she was ill. If I'd have known, I would have called for help sooner. It wasn't my fault."

He held up a hand. "I'm Detective Dalton Vail. Please tell me what happened from the start, Miss Shore." When she'd finished, he studied his notes. "Let's see if I've got this straight. You wrapped her hair, gave her a cup of coffee, then went into the back room. Hearing a noise, you returned to find the woman slumped in the chair."

Marla nodded. "That's right." Her knees weakening, she sank onto a seat at the closest hair station. A quick glance in the mirror unsettled her. Her shiny chestnut hair curled inward at chin length, wispy bangs feathering a forehead creased with worry lines. A stranger's fearful eyes, dark as toffee, stared back at her. Surely, that ghastly complexion couldn't be hers. She looked ill, which was certainly how she felt, but this wasn't as horrible as that day when—

"You made a fresh pot of coffee just before Mrs. Kravitz came in?" Detective Vail asked, ripping her away from painful memories.

She nodded, glad for the distraction. "I poured some coffee into her mug, then added a package of sugar and two spoonfuls of powdered creamer. My other customers prefer Half & Half, but Bertha insisted on using the dry variety. I kept a jar just for her."

A gleam entered his gray eyes. "Where is it?"

"I'm afraid I threw it out. I'd used up the last amount. She said the coffee tasted bitter," Marla recalled. "I didn't think much of it because she complained about everything."

"Did you notice the color of the creamer?"

"Not really."

"Any unusual odors?"

"No… yes. I did smell something after Mrs. Kravitz… when I went to feel her pulse. It reminded me of"—she wrinkled her nose—"marzipan. Yes, that's it."

His eyes narrowed. "You mean almonds?"

"I believe so."

He scanned the tabletop holding the coffeemaker and related supplies. "Where do you normally keep the foodstuffs?"

"In a rear storeroom."

"Who's allowed back there?"

"Mainly the staff, but sometimes a client will wander inside to take a look. The door is always open."

"You said the creamer jar was nearly empty. Did you recall using most of it the last time the lady was here?"

"Not really." An idea dawned on her that made her pulse accelerate. "Surely you don't think it was something in her drink?"

"We're just collecting evidence, ma'am. The medical examiner will determine cause of death. Is there anything else that might be relevant?"

She frowned. "The back door was unlocked when I

arrived this morning. I meant to speak to the cleaning crew about it later."

"I see. Please excuse me." He held a hushed conference with two techs, one of whom veered off to examine the trash and another who headed for the rear entrance. They'd already scooped up the dribbled remains of coffee on the floor, collected pieces of the broken mug, and dusted everything for fingerprints. The medical examiner had taken charge of the body. Finished with his initial assessment, he'd called the removal service.

*Please get here soon*, Marla thought, looking everywhere but at the dead woman. To distract herself, she calculated the cost of a new shampoo chair.

Vail returned to resume his interview. "Tell me, how would you describe your relationship with Bertha Kravitz?"

She compressed her lips. "She was a regular client."

"When did she start coming here to get her hair done?"

"Ever since I opened the shop, eight years ago."

"Did you know her before that time?"

Marla hesitated a fraction too long. "Sure," she said, careful to keep her tone casual. "I'd met her at local charity events."

**ORDER NOW** at
https://nancyjcohen.com/permed-to-death/

# BREADS

# BANANA BRAN MUFFINS

*If you're watching your weight, these are great muffins to make from scratch. They're low in calories and are good for breakfast with some fruit or yogurt on the side. Or eat one as a healthy snack. You can also cut a muffin in half and put jam on the layers for more moisture.*

## Ingredients

2 ripe bananas, peeled
$1^1/_4$ cups skim milk
2 egg whites
2 Tbsp. applesauce
$2^1/_4$ cups oat bran hot cereal, uncooked
1 Tbsp. baking powder
$^1/_4$ cup dark brown sugar
$^1/_4$ cup chopped walnuts

## Directions

Preheat oven to 425 degrees. In a blender, mash bananas. Add milk, egg whites, and applesauce. Blend together. Meanwhile, mix the dry ingredients in a large bowl. Add milk mixture and stir. Optional: add dried fruit, i.e. dried cranberries, raisins or chopped dates. Grease muffin pan with non-stick spray or line with paper baking cups. Fill each cup about 3/4 full with batter. Bake for 17 minutes. Makes 12 muffins.

# CORN MUFFINS

*These are easy to make and welcome at a dinner party or holiday meal. This recipe came from my cousin Julia, who doesn't entertain the family often. When she does, she takes the easiest route to cooking with the least preparation possible. She'd rather watch her nail polish dry than spend time in the kitchen.*

## Ingredients

17 oz. can of corn
$^1/_4$ cup melted butter
2 cups biscuit mix
$^1/_3$ cup nonfat dry milk
3 Tbsp. sugar
1 cup shredded cheddar cheese
1 egg, beaten
2 Tbsp. chopped onion
$^1/_4$ tsp. dried dill
Pinch of dried thyme

## Directions

Preheat oven to 400 degrees. Drain corn, reserving liquid. Add liquid to melted butter to measure $^2/_3$ cup of liquid total. Combine biscuit mix, dry milk, and sugar in a large bowl. Stir in corn, cheese, beaten egg, liquid, onion, dill, and thyme. Stir to blend. Fill greased muffin cups 2/3 full. Bake for 25 minutes. Makes 12 muffins.

# CRANBERRY BREAD

*This recipe is a no-brainer for Thanksgiving. I prefer using fresh cranberries in a recipe when available. We'll refrigerate leftovers to eat a slice for breakfast later along with a hard-boiled egg for protein.*

## Ingredients

2 cups all-purpose unbleached flour
1 cup light brown sugar
$1/_2$ tsp. baking soda
$1^1/_2$ tsp. baking powder
1 tsp. salt
4 Tbsp. unsalted butter, melted
1 large egg, lightly beaten
$3/_4$ cup whole milk
12 oz. bag fresh cranberries
Cinnamon Sugar

## Directions

Preheat oven to 350 degrees. Grease and flour a loaf pan. In a large bowl, mix flour, sugar, baking soda, baking powder, and salt. In a medium bowl, stir together melted butter, egg, and milk. Add liquids to flour mixture. Stir to combine, then fold in cranberries. Put batter into prepared loaf pan. Sprinkle cinnamon sugar on top. Bake for 1 hour or until toothpick comes out clean. Cool briefly on rack, then slice and serve.

Nancy J. Cohen

# GARLIC CHEESE BISCUITS

*I'll have to admit that I'm a sucker for the cheesy biscuits
served at a local chain seafood restaurant. These are a
substitute, although you can now buy the mix directly from
this brand in the supermarket. Dalton isn't much of a fan, but
Brianna gobbles them up reheated in the microwave as an
after-school snack.*

**Ingredients**

2 cups biscuit mix
$^1/_2$ cup shredded cheddar cheese
2 cloves garlic, minced
$^2/_3$ cup low fat milk
2 Tbsp. butter, melted
$^1/_4$ tsp. garlic powder

**Directions**

Preheat oven to 450 degrees. Combine biscuit mix, shredded
cheese, and minced garlic in a large bowl. Stir in milk until
moistened. Drop by the tablespoon onto a greased cookie
sheet. Bake for 10 minutes or until browned. Meanwhile, mix
together melted butter and garlic powder. Brush over warm
biscuits and serve. Makes 12 biscuits.

# LYCHEE BLUEBERRY MUFFINS

*When my parents first moved to Florida from New York State, my father planted a lychee tree along with lemon and tangelo trees on their property. The lychee outlasted the other two that died out due to some disease that was not citrus canker. The lychee grew so tall that they had to cut it down eventually, because they kept having to clean out fallen leaves from the house's gutters. When the tree fruited and before the branches got too tall to reach, they harvested the bristly red fruits. My brother and I had fun peeling off the outer skins and sucking the pulp around the seed. Fresh lychees are incredibly sweet with a unique taste. My mother harvested bowls full, so she created recipes to use the abundant fruit.*

## Ingredients

2 cups unbleached flour
1 Tbsp. baking powder
1 tsp. ground cinnamon
$1/4$ tsp. freshly grated nutmeg
$1/4$ tsp. salt
2 eggs
1 cup reduced fat milk
$1/4$ cup canola oil
$1/2$ cup brown sugar
1 tsp. vanilla
2 Tbsp. applesauce
$1/3$ cup fresh lychees, chopped and drained
$1/4$ cup fresh blueberries

**Directions**

Preheat oven to 350 degrees. Grease a muffin tin. In a large bowl, mix the flour, baking powder, cinnamon, nutmeg, and salt. In a medium bowl, beat the eggs, milk, oil, brown sugar, vanilla, and applesauce until smooth. Stir liquid mixture into dry ingredients. Add lychees and blueberries and mix until blended.

Fill each muffin cup about 3/4 full. Bake for 20 to 25 minutes or until lightly browned and a toothpick inserted in the center comes out clean. Cool on rack when done. Makes 12 muffins.

# RITZ CRACKER STUFFING

*My mother inherited this recipe from my grandmother, and Ma always serves it with our Thanksgiving turkey dinner. It's still my favorite over stuffing made with bread. I like it so much that I'll eat the leftovers for a snack.*

## Ingredients

3 or more rolls of Ritz Crackers, crushed
2 eggs or $1/2$ cup egg substitute
2 Tbsp. olive oil
1 onion, chopped
8 oz. container chopped celery
8 oz. bag shredded carrots
Garlic powder
Salt to taste
Dry white wine

## Directions

Preheat oven to 350 degrees. Crumple crackers into a large bowl. Add eggs, mix to blend, and set aside. In a frypan, sauté chopped onions and celery in olive oil until wilted. Add to crackers along with shredded carrots. Sprinkle in garlic powder and salt to taste. Add enough white wine to moisten the mixture. Transfer stuffing to a greased 2-quart casserole dish and bake for 20 to 30 minutes or until edges are browned and mixture is heated through. Serves 6 to 8.

# FACIALS CAN BE FATAL

## Bad Hair Day Mystery #13

*Although* Facials Can Be Fatal *does not contain recipes, it reveals some interesting information about an additive in breads that relates to hair.*

### The Story

Salon owner Marla Vail's new day spa hits a snag when a client dies during a facial. The victim, Valerie Weston, was a major donor for Friends of Old Florida, a historic building preservation society. Marla's stylists are scheduled to work backstage at their upcoming fashion show, but Val's demise might put a crimp in their plans. Hoping to salvage her reputation, Marla determines to track down the killer. As she learns more about Val, she realizes the benefactress might have stumbled onto secrets others would kill to keep. She'd better prepare for a body count that has nothing to do with hot stone massages and everything to do with murder.

### Excerpt from Facials Can Be Fatal

When Nicole asked her for the latest news on the case, Marla felt comfortable talking to her. They had a moment in between clients, and she wanted to share what she had learned.

"Ugh, that's awful," Nicole said, her nose scrunching. "He cuts hair from dead people and sells them for extensions?"

"I suspect Gabriel Stone sells the hair to Henutt who ships it to China. From what I've read online, the United States, Britain, and China are the three major world buyers. Forty percent of the hair sold is made into extensions."

Nicole stuck a comb into the Barbicide jar. "So what's done with the rest?"

Standing by her station, Marla looked up the notes she'd written on her smartphone. "Shorter hair from men is used by chemical companies. The amino acids in hair have multiple industrial uses, including food additives. It's cheaper than synthetic sources."

"Eww. How would I know I'm eating it?"

"Look for an ingredient labeled L-cysteine. It can be used to leaven bread, for example." Marla read from her notes. "Human hair is first dissolved in acid. The L-cysteine, isolated by a chemical process, is packaged and shipped to commercial bread makers. Other sources of this amino acid include chicken or duck feathers and petroleum by-products."

"That's disgusting."

"Listen to this. Most of the hair used to make the L-cysteine comes from the floors of barbershops and hair salons in China. There's also a temple in India where people donate their hair to their god as an act of humility. They shave your head, then women sweep it up and throw it into a giant steel vat. It gets sold at auction to the international market."

Nicole stared at the strands of hair littering their floor, the remnants of haircuts that the assistant had yet to sweep up. "So you're saying we're standing on a gold mine."

"So to speak. I've even read reports of Russian prisoners having their heads shaved against their will, and the harvesting of hair from corpses."

"Gross. I don't think I'll buy baked goods anymore."

"It's also a flavor enhancer and may have other uses in the food industry."

"So how can you tell where the L-cysteine ingredient comes from, whether it's animal in origin or synthetic?"

"There isn't any way to tell if it's not on the label. If you're concerned, I'd suggest trying kosher goods or vegan items. They'd be a safer bet. Hey, get this. Blonde is the most popular color for the human hair trade because it can be dyed more easily. Wavy hair has the best-selling texture."

"I think I've learned more than I wanted to know, thanks."

"Don't you agree this all fits? Henutt is buying hair from Stone and shipping it to China."

Nicole tilted her head. "So you think Valerie Weston somehow discovered their scheme and they killed her over it?"

"It's a distinct possibility, at least where Henutt is concerned."

**ORDER NOW** at

https://nancyjcohen.com/facials-can-be-fatal/

# SAUCES

# CRANBERRY SAUCE

*This is so much better than buying the alternative in a can. Cranberry sauce and turkey go together like peanut butter and jelly, but it's always best when you can make your own.*

## Ingredients

12 oz. bag fresh cranberries
$3/4$ cup sugar
1 tsp. grated lemon peel
1 cup water

## Directions

In a medium pot, mix all ingredients. Bring to a boil then reduce heat and simmer about 10 minutes or until cranberries are softened. Cool, transfer to serving dish, and store covered in refrigerator until served.

Nancy J. Cohen

# TURKEY GRAVY

*My grandmother used the giblets, I think she called them, and other bony parts from animal carcasses when she cooked. I'm not fond of organs that way, but this is a fairly easy recipe if you want to make use of the innards from your turkey.*

## Ingredients

2 Tbsp. canola oil
Turkey neck bone
2 medium carrots, chopped
1 large onion, chopped
32 oz. low sodium chicken broth
1 Tbsp. chopped fresh parsley
1 Tbsp. minced fresh sage
1 tsp. dried thyme
2 bay leaves
$1/_4$ cup cornstarch
$1/_4$ cup cold water
Salt to taste

## Directions

In a Dutch oven, heat oil. Add turkey neck bone and brown on all sides. Remove from pan. Add the carrots and onion. Sauté until wilted and lightly browned. Return turkey part to pan. Add chicken broth, parsley, sage, thyme and bay leaves. Cover and simmer for 30 minutes.

When done, strain gravy through a fine mesh strainer and return to pot. In a small bowl, whisk together the cornstarch and water. Add to broth, increase heat, and whisk until thickened and bubbly. Ladle into gravy boat and serve with turkey.

# WHITE WINE GRAVY

*Charlene, my brother Michael's wife, makes this simple gravy when she's on the run from her job as schoolteacher and mother of two kids. She doesn't host our holiday dinners often, preferring to let the rest of us handle the details. But on occasion, she'll roast a turkey and then this is her go-to recipe for gravy.*

## Ingredients

3 Tbsp. cornstarch
³/₄ cup dry white wine
1 chicken bouillon cube
¹/₄ cup sliced green onions
Pan juices from roasted turkey

## Directions

Skim fat from pan turkey juices. Pour remaining juice into measuring cup. Add water to make 2 cups of liquid. In a medium saucepan, blend the cornstarch and the white wine. Add pan juices, a chicken bouillon cube, and ¼ cup sliced green onions. Cook and stir until thick and bubbly. Add salt to taste. Ladle into gravy boat and serve with turkey.

# HAIR RAISER

## Bad Hair Day Mystery #2

Hair Raiser *doesn't contain recipes, but the story centers around a Taste of the World fundraiser involving a roster of chefs and including various food scenes.*

### The Story

When South Florida hairstylist Marla Shore takes charge of a fundraiser for a coastal preservation society, she has to comb through a knot of suspects to determine who's sabotaging their gala event. Participating chefs are dropping off the roster like hot rollers, and it's only through a series of hair-raising exploits that she can tease the truth from a tangle of suspects. Too late to stop a murder, Marla must salvage the grand affair before she's moussed into oblivion.

### Excerpt from Hair Raiser

"Let's go have dessert over at the Seafood Emporium," Marla suggested after she and Nicole had both finished a generous portion of moussaka. When their attentive waiter approached holding out a platter with a delectable array of sweets, she shook her head, declining the temptation of a syrupy slice of baklava. "We're not far from the other restaurant, so we might as well stop in there to see Max. He's next on my list."

"Hey, girl, I'm going to get fat going out with you," Nicole complained.

Marla pretended to scrutinize her friend's narrow waistline. "I don't think so. You're one of those disgusting people who never gains weight."

Max was preparing a sauce to go with grilled trout when they entered his kitchen. "Hey, ladies," the lean young man said while he whisked cream into a boiling mixture of dry white wine, balsamic vinegar, and minced shallots. When the cream had blended in, he added diced tomatoes. Marla recognized the ingredients from her gourmet cooking days when she was married to Stan. Now she had little time to cook, let alone follow recipes.

"This is Nicole. We stopped in for some dessert," Marla explained. "As long as we're here, I'd like to confirm your arrangements for Taste of the World."

Max cut a chunk of butter into the sauce, his wrist rotating with rapid, deft movements. "Everything is fine." A curl of hair fell forward onto his forehead as he bent over to sniff the aroma emanating from the pan.

"You haven't heard from anyone else about the event?"

"Nope. Been too busy." He cast a furtive glance around the room. "You gals will have to excuse me, but I don't have time to chat. We're short one cook tonight, and I've got to do my own prep work. Y'all go on and enjoy your dessert."

He walked away from them, ostensibly to get some ingredients to add to his dish, but Marla had the distinct impression they were being dismissed. Was he being less talkative than usual because others were present? Maybe she'd corner him another time when they could be alone.

After dropping Nicole off at home, she decided to make one more stop before turning in for the night. Saturday was too good an opportunity to miss since all the chefs were at work. Robbie from the Cajun Cookpot hadn't responded to her latest inquiry. It was worth driving to Davie to ask why he hadn't contacted her.

Too stuffed to order any more meals, she skirted the front door and headed for an employee entrance down a side alley. As she approached, the smell of garbage overwhelmed her. An open trash bin stood outside the kitchen door, its contents spilling beyond the rim. Insects flew in and out the open door to the kitchen, from which came the sounds of clanging pots and pans. *Yuck,* Marla thought. *I wonder what else is crawling around inside there.*

Squaring her shoulders, she marched inside. A spicy scent made her eyes water. Several workers looked up, their expressions startled. She braced herself to meet Robbie, who was bound to be displeased by her unexpected arrival.

"What are you doing here?" he thundered when he caught sight of her. He was stirring the contents of a giant pot, his thick neck veins bulging, biceps straining under his soiled white jacket. Dipping a spoon into the pot, he raised it to his lips and slurped the hot steamy liquid. He cursed, grabbed a fistful of cayenne pepper and tossed it into the pot. Stirring vigorously, he regarded Marla with a glower.

She smiled with a bravado she didn't feel, uneasy at the leers from his employees. "I'm wondering why you didn't return my form for Taste of the World. Have you selected your menu items? It's getting near time when we have to send out new press releases."

"Get me some more tomatoes, will ya?" he hollered to an assistant. The man glanced up but didn't respond. "Whatsamatta, you no speaky English? Grab me a bunch of those red tomatoes," he shouted as though the guy were deaf. "Christ, this help ain't worth shit." He got up and grabbed the items himself. Reaching for a long knife, he began slicing the plump tomatoes on a wooden cutting board.

"Well? What about the form?" Marla said, tapping her foot impatiently. Frustration made her breath come short, or maybe it was the lack of air-conditioning. A fan blew moist air around the kitchen, but it didn't do much to pull in a breeze from the alley. The garbage-scented breeze, she remembered, wrinkling her nose. Her sweater stuck to her back, and she longed for a cool drink.

"I'll get to it one of these days." Robbie spied a roach scurrying away on the counter. He leapt at it, steel blade slashing through the air. After he'd reduced the creature to pieces, he brushed the remains onto the floor and continued slicing the tomatoes.

Marla stifled an impulse to gag. Her gaze fixed on the pot of bubbling stew, circled by a duo of insects. "Maybe you should take your time. I might want to mention these unsanitary conditions to the restaurant inspectors."

Straightening his back, Robbie glared at her. "You do and you're dead."

*If your restaurant weren't so popular, I'd take you off my list right now. Dirty scumbag.* Maybe she'd eliminate him anyway. He was never in a pleasant mood and ran his kitchen like a sewer. She'd have to be careful how she justified herself to Ocean Guard's Board of Directors, though. Robbie wasn't the type of person you wanted to cross.

"Time for you to leave," he ordered.

"But we haven't—"

He brandished his knife, stalking toward her with a menacing light in his eyes. "Get out."

Marla stumbled into the alley. The chef slammed the door after her. It didn't even shut properly; the warped wood prevented closure. Her limbs trembling, she recovered her wits enough to scramble to her car.

*I'm just like that roach scampering away; only it had ended up getting diced to death.*

**ORDER NOW** at
https://nancyjcohen.com/hair-raiser/

51

# SOUPS

# BUTTERNUT SQUASH SOUP

*Dalton and I have taken the occasional cooking class, and this is a delicious recipe I'd gleaned from the Thanksgiving-themed one. It's a rich, buttery soup that will have you asking for more. Using freshly grated nutmeg is a must for the full taste to come through. Ma bought me a nutmeg grater with a bag of fresh nuts when she cruised to Grenada, and I've been hooked on using the fresh ingredient rather than the jar variety ever since then.*

## Ingredients

2 Tbsp. butter
1 onion, diced
1 pound peeled and cubed butternut squash
1 carrot, sliced
$\frac{1}{4}$ tsp. cinnamon
$\frac{1}{4}$ tsp. freshly grated nutmeg
Pinch ground cloves
32 oz. low sodium chicken broth
2 sprigs thyme
2 Tbsp. unsulphured molasses
1 cup half-and-half

## Directions

Melt butter over medium heat in large soup pot. Add onion and cook until translucent. Then add squash and carrots. Cook for 4 to 5 minutes, stirring often. Add spices and cook until vegetables start to caramelize. Add chicken broth and thyme. Simmer for 20 minutes.

Remove from heat and discard thyme sprigs. Using an immersion blender, puree the soup. (It can be frozen at this stage.) Stir in molasses to blend. Add half-and-half and mix to combine. Ladle into individual bowls and serve hot.

If frozen, defrost gradually and then reheat in large pot. Stir in molasses and half-and-half and serve as above.

# FRENCH ONION SOUP

*This recipe came from a cooking class I had taken in the early days when I was dating Stan. My ex had a finely tuned palate, and I meant to impress him with my French cuisine skills in the kitchen. However, I made one major mistake. I totally forgot to add the onions. Oops! You can make a meal of this soup along with a salad.*

## Ingredients

$1/4$ cup butter
5 cups thinly sliced onions
$1/4$ tsp. sugar
1 cup red wine
(4) 10.5 oz. cans condensed beef broth, undiluted
4 to 6 French bread slices, each one inch thick
1 cup grated Swiss cheese
Olive oil

## Directions

Preheat oven to 325 degrees. Melt butter in large soup pot. Add onions, stir, and simmer, covered, until golden, about 15 minutes, stirring occasionally. Uncover, raise heat to medium, and stir in sugar. Cook 10 minutes. Add red wine and beef broth, bring to boil. Reduce heat and simmer for 30 minutes. (Can freeze soup at this stage if desired).

Meanwhile, toast bread slices until browned on both sides. Sprinkle each slice of bread with grated cheese and a few drops of olive oil on top. Pour soup into oven-proof tureens. Float toast, cheese side up, one slice in each bowl. Bake for 20 minutes, then put under broiler for a minute or until top is browned and bubbly. Serve immediately, or cool and refrigerate, covered. May be reheated in oven.

# MINESTRONE SOUP

*Most people like a good vegetable soup, and this is both healthy and easy to make. Throw all the ingredients into a soup pot and bring to a low boil. You can use any kind of pasta that you have in stock or leave it out entirely. As for vegetables, if you have favorites, add them in or substitute for items below. For extra flavor, toss in a piece of Parmesan rind to the soup.*

## Ingredients

48 oz. low sodium chicken broth
28 oz. can petite diced tomatoes, undrained
15 oz. can whole white potatoes, drained and halved
15.5 oz. can cannellini beans, drained and rinsed
9 oz. package frozen cut green beans
8 oz. package shredded carrots
1 large onion, cut into chunks
$1/4$ red bell pepper, diced
2 Tbsp. chopped fresh parsley
1 Tbsp. chopped fresh dill
$3/4$ cup Ditalini pasta

## Directions

Combine all ingredients except pasta in large soup pot and bring to a boil. Cover and simmer for 30 minutes. Add pasta and cook for additional 10 minutes. Ladle into individual bowls and serve hot.

# MUSHROOM BARLEY SOUP

*Aunt Selma used to make this tasty mushroom barley soup when we visited her apartment in New York, before she and Uncle Moishe moved to Denver. You could smell it down the hallway. Uncle Moishe ate it for a meal along with rye bread and butter. He'd eat this in the winter and red beet borsht in the summer. No wonder he stayed so thin. Whenever I make this soup, the aroma reminds me of my aunt and uncle.*

## Ingredients

1 Tbsp. olive oil
8 oz. chopped onions
24 oz. sliced mushrooms
2 tsp. chopped garlic
$1/4$ cup chopped fresh parsley
$1/4$ tsp. dried thyme
$1/4$ cup chopped fresh dill
$4 1/2$ cups low sodium chicken broth
2 cups water
1 cup quick-cooking barley

## Directions

Heat olive oil in soup pot. Sauté onions, mushrooms, and garlic until wilted. Add parsley, thyme, and dill. Stir in chicken broth and 2 cups water. Mix in barley. Bring to a boil then lower heat to simmer. Cook until barley is tender and flavors blend, about 15 minutes. Ladle into individual bowls and serve hot.

# POTATO LEEK SOUP

*This is like a vichyssoise soup from my French cooking days but an easier version. It makes a nice starter course for a dinner party.*

## Ingredients

2 Tbsp. butter
2 leeks
3 medium potatoes, peeled and cut in chunks. Keep in cold water until used.
3 cups low sodium chicken broth
2 cups water
1 bunch watercress, stemmed and rinsed
1 cup heavy cream or evaporated skim milk

## Directions

Trim ends and outer green stalks from leeks. Rinse layers, chop on cutting board, then rinse again in colander. Heat the butter in a saucepan to melt. Add leeks and sauté until wilted. Add potatoes, broth, and water. Bring to a boil and simmer for 30 minutes. Add watercress and simmer for another 20 minutes.

Remove from heat, allow soup to cool briefly, and then blend with immersion blender. Stir in cream and reheat, or refrigerate and serve cold.

# SWEET ONION CHOWDER

*I had a similar soup when driving through Georgia once and stopping for lunch at a Southern-style buffet. The food was amazing. If I ate like that every day, I'd be as big as a bouffant hairdo in my mid-section. I adapted this recipe from one for Vidalia onions. It's great to make when large sweet onions are in season. Add more broth if you want added liquid. You can also leave out the cream as an option.*

## Ingredients

$1/4$ cup butter
4 to 5 large sweet onions, peeled and sliced
1 tsp. sugar
1 Tbsp. chopped fresh dill
11 oz. can white corn, drained
48 oz. low sodium chicken broth
2 Tbsp. flour
$1/2$ cup half-and-half

## Directions

Melt butter in soup pot. Add onions. Stir and simmer, covered, on medium heat until softened, about 20 minutes. Sprinkle in the sugar and mix again, cooking a few more minutes. Then add dill and corn. In a separate bowl, whisk flour into broth to blend. Pour into pot and whisk until smooth. Heat to a boil and simmer for 10 to 20 minutes, stirring occasionally.

Remove from heat and gently stir in half-and-half. Ladle into individual bowls and serve hot.

# TOMATO BISQUE

*The immersion blender is one of the best kitchen tools invented. I love to use it for soups. This tomato bisque goes great with a grilled cheese sandwich.*

## Ingredients

3 Tbsp. olive oil
1 large onion, chopped
8 oz. celery, chopped
1 Tbsp. tomato paste
3 cups low sodium chicken broth
$1/_2$ cup white wine
1 Tbsp. chopped garlic
1 cup baby carrots
0.75 oz. package fresh basil, trimmed
28 oz. can low sodium tomatoes, undrained
$1/_3$ cup whipping cream

## Directions

In a large soup pot, sauté onions and celery in olive oil until wilted. Mix in tomato paste. Add chicken broth, wine, garlic, carrots, basil and tomatoes. Simmer for 30 minutes.

Remove from heat and gently stir in whipping cream. Blend with immersion blender. Add salt to taste. Ladle into individual bowls and serve hot.

Nancy J. Cohen

# TOMATO LENTIL SOUP

*I acquired this recipe from Dalton's mom, Kate. She manages to prepare dinner for a crowd in her small condo kitchen. She's not a vegetarian, but Kate and John both try to avoid red meat and eat healthy choices. This may be how they stay trim since neither of them exercises on a regular basis.*

*Regarding type of lentils, choose your own. I use Publix lentils from the local supermarket. They do not require soaking and are greenish-brown in color. The label does not mention a variety. So if you have a particular preference, try it in this recipe. Make sure the lentils don't need pre-soaking.*

## Ingredients

4$^1/_2$ cups water
8 oz. fresh sliced carrots
1 cup chopped onions
$^2/_3$ cup dried lentils, rinsed
6 oz. can tomato paste
1 Tbsp. brown sugar
1 tsp. garlic powder
2 Tbsp. chopped fresh parsley
$^1/_2$ tsp. dried thyme
$^1/_4$ tsp. dried dill
1 Tbsp. white vinegar

## Directions

In a large pot, combine water, carrots, onions and lentils, and bring to a boil. Cover and simmer for 20 minutes or until vegetables are tender. Stir in the remaining ingredients. Ladle into individual bowls and serve hot.

# TURKEY SOUP

*This is an easy but yummy soup to make after a holiday meal. Throw in whatever vegetables you have on hand. Either serve the soup as is, or use an immersion blender. It's so good that I can't wait for the next turkey feast to make it again.*

## Ingredients

1 leftover turkey carcass
10 cups water
2 celery ribs, cut into chunks with celery leaves
1 large onion, cut into chunks
1 handful of fresh thyme sprigs
1 package baby spinach
15.5 oz. can low sodium great northern beans, drained and rinsed
8 oz. baby carrots
8 oz. fresh sliced mushrooms
2 chicken bouillon cubes

## Directions

Put the turkey carcass in a soup pot and add water. Toss in celery, onion and thyme. Bring to a boil. Lower heat, cover and simmer for 2 hours.

Remove carcass, all remaining bones, and thyme sprigs. Strain through a fine mesh sieve to remove solids. Take off any meat from the bones and add back to soup. Add spinach, beans, carrots, mushrooms and bouillon cubes. Simmer covered for another 30 minutes. Ladle into individual bowls and serve hot.

# VEGETABLE BEAN SOUP

*This is my version of the soup below that my grandmother used to make using beef marrow bones. I prefer to prepare it using vegetables only, and it comes out tasting almost as good. I have to admit the bones and marrow give it a richer flavor, but this version is healthier by my standards. It freezes well and is a good choice for chilly winter weather. If you have other vegetables in stock, either toss them in or substitute for items below.*

## Ingredients

$3/4$ cup dried large lima beans
(2) 48 oz. boxes low sodium chicken broth
2 cups water
9 oz. package fresh spinach
0.75 package fresh basil, trimmed
Handful each of fresh dill and parsley, chopped
1 turnip, peeled and cut into chunks
1 parsnip, peeled and cut into chunks
1 large onion cut into chunks
8 oz. baby carrots
$1/4$ cup barley
$1/4$ cup dried split peas
15.5 oz. can cannellini beans, drained and rinsed
14.5 oz. can diced tomatoes, undrained

## Directions

The day before, cover dried lima beans with boiling water in a bowl and refrigerate overnight. In the morning, peel and discard skins. Set lima beans aside. Trim stems on fresh herbs. Bring broth and water to a boil in a large soup pot. Add spinach. Stir until spinach is wilted, then add other ingredients. Cover pot with one side partially open to vent and simmer for two hours.

Remove from heat and cool slightly, then blend all ingredients with immersion blender. Ladle into individual soup bowls and serve hot. Soup can be divided into smaller portions and frozen for later use.

# VEGETABLE BARLEY SOUP

*This is the heartier version of the soup above. I watched my grandmother make it, trying it a few times for myself once I had my own kitchen. You can buy the marrow bones in the supermarket in the meat section. I suppose you get some health benefits from the marrow but it's also a beef product, so if you prefer your soup to be vegetarian, make the version above. If you like a richer soup, try this one. For even more flavor, roast the bones in a 350 degree oven until brown then proceed as below. This soup freezes well after it cools.*

## Ingredients

$3/_4$ cup dried large lima beans
3 to 5 beef marrow bones, depending on size
1 bunch fresh celery leaves
$1/_4$ cup dried split peas
1 Tbsp. each fresh parsley and dill, chopped
$1/_4$ cup pearl barley
$1/_4$ cup uncooked rice
8 oz. baby carrots
1 large onion, peeled
1 parsnip, peeled
1 turnip, peeled
1 small potato, peeled
1 soft tomato
4 oz. fresh sliced mushrooms

## Directions

The day before, cover dried lima beans with boiling water in a bowl and refrigerate overnight. In the morning, peel and discard skins. Set lima beans aside. Rinse marrow bones and place in bottom of large soup pot. Cover with cold water and bring to a boil. Skim foam off top. Lower heat and add all other ingredients. Simmer covered for about two hours, stirring occasionally, until all vegetables are tender.

Remove from heat and let soup cool slightly while uncovered. With a slotted spoon, remove marrow bones. Shake out marrow from bones into soup. Discard bones. Use immersion blender to puree soup until thoroughly blended. Ladle into individual bowls and serve hot.

# HAUNTED HAIR NIGHTS

## Bad Hair Day Mystery #12.5

Haunted Hair Nights *doesn't have recipes, but it does have a scene where Marla orders a bowl of soup while questioning suspects. Food is often a part of social gatherings or important meetings. In this instance, she might learn something new that could help her husband solve his latest murder case.*

**The Story**

Hairstylist Marla Vail hopes to win brownie points by helping her stepdaughter with a school haunted house project. All goes well until Marla stumbles over a corpse on the spooky estate grounds. Between slacker students, helicopter parents, unexpected heirs, and a stonewalling school administration, Marla has her hands full in solving the murder and keeping the kids safe. Can she sift through the suspects and unmask the killer before Halloween fright night turns into reality?

**Excerpt from Haunted Hair Nights**

Marla recognized some of the faces among a group of youths, but no way could she barge in there as a lone adult. What was the best way to make her approach?

Brianna tugged on her arm. "Come on. I know these kids."

From the girl's terse voice, Marla surmised this was difficult for her as well. She dutifully followed along, drawing over a chair in imitation of the teen's action.

"Hey, guys. This is my stepmom, Marla. She's absolutely starving, so I thought we'd stop by here. What's good to eat?"

"I like the burgers and milkshakes," said one girl. While Brianna engaged her in conversation, Marla waved to Jules, whom she remembered from the haunted house. He had the complexion of a ghost, as though he hibernated indoors during the school year.

"Hi, I remember you from Mr. Ripari's house," she called to him. "That was a terrible night."

"Rest in peace, Mr. R-I-P Ripari," sneered a youth at his side. This kid had a snub nose, a broad forehead, and a head of thick black hair. He regarded Marla with an unfriendly stare.

"I'm sorry, we haven't met," she said to him.

Jules responded. "This is my friend, Patrick." He nudged the guy. "Mrs. Vail is married to a cop. Brie's dad is a police detective."

Did Marla detect a note of warning in his tone? "That's right. I've heard Mr. Ripari was tutoring you in history, Patrick. I know Ricky had some trouble in his class and was wondering why he didn't get help after hours."

"Ricky wouldn't put up with his shit."

Marla, taken aback by the vehemence in Patrick's tone, couldn't immediately think of a comeback. "Didn't Mr. Ripari help you as a tutor?" she asked after a moment.

"He helped himself more than he did me."

Jules poked him again. "Patrick, be careful what you say. The man is gone. He can't hurt anybody now."

Marla pounced on his words. "The teacher hurt you? In what way?"

Patrick shot her a hooded glance. "What's it to you?"

"I'm a concerned parent, especially if a student is harmed."

"Well, don't be. Like the dumb principal would do anything in this case. He wants Mr. Ripari's property too badly. Principal Underwood would brag about how they were friends and how the history teacher's will favored the school." He snickered. "I know what kind of *friends* they were."

71

Oh, my. Marla got an inkling of what he meant, and it made sense on many levels. But how could she get one of these people to come out and say it?

"Hey, here comes the deadly duo," Jules proclaimed. His fingers drummed on the table, adding to his jerky motions. The guy couldn't seem to sit still. His gaze darted about the room like a hunted rabbit.

Marla raised her head as a pair of girls arrived, ogling the fellows. Brianna came to her rescue, introducing Maya and Rose. The former barely covered her skin in a skimpy outfit and oozed sex appeal in the way she moved, while Rose dressed more demurely. Rose kissed a buff fellow on the lips. Oh, yes. Wasn't that Shaun from the football team?

"Hi, Rose. Good to see you again. We met at the haunted house."

The girl gave a nervous glance at the others. "Oh, right. How are you, Mrs. Vail?"

"I'm good, thanks." The waitress interrupted, and Marla placed her order for a bowl of mushroom barley soup. She sat back to listen as the teens engaged in school chitchat. Brianna held her own with this bunch, but it clearly wasn't her normal crowd. She kept glancing at the entrance as though wishing she were elsewhere.

Feeling like an outsider as well, Marla had a sudden revelation that took her breath away. Aside from Brianna, didn't all of these kids have a reason to resent Mr. Ripari?

**ORDER NOW** at
https://nancyjcohen.com/haunted-hair-nights/

# ENTREES — BEEF

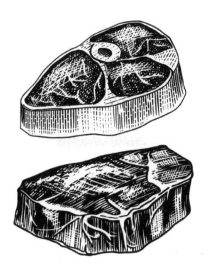

# BEEFY MACARONI & CHEESE

*This choice is comfort food at its best. It's quick to prepare after work and satisfying to the stomach. If you prefer, use your own homemade macaroni and cheese recipe. I use a box mix for convenience. This dish is still tasty when reheated as leftovers for dinner the next night.*

## Ingredients

14.5 oz. family-size box Kraft Original Macaroni & Cheese Dinner
8 cups water
4 Tbsp. unsalted butter
$1/2$ cup fat free milk
1 pound lean ground beef
$1/2$ tsp. minced garlic
14.5 oz. can no salt added petite diced tomatoes
$1^1/_4$ cups tomato basil spaghetti sauce
1 to 2 cups shredded mozzarella cheese

## Directions

Preheat oven to 350 degrees. Prepare macaroni and cheese dinner according to package directions for lighter prep using fat free milk and 4 Tbsp. butter as above. Set aside. Meanwhile, sauté beef and garlic in non-stick skillet until browned. Remove from pan. Mix together diced tomatoes with juice and spaghetti sauce to make 3 cups total.

In a greased 9-inch square baking dish, layer the macaroni mixture, sauce, meat, and mozzarella cheese. Bake until browned and heated through, about 20 minutes. Serves 6 to 8.

# BRISKET COLA

*Cousin Cynthia served this for Rosh Hashanah one season, and I was hooked. It's the best brisket ever and so easy to put together. My mother gave me her cast iron Dutch oven, and that's what I use to slow cook this meat in the oven at a low temperature. The brisket comes out very tender with a rich flavor and is a great company dish.*

## Ingredients

3 to 4 pounds flat cut beef brisket
2 Tbsp. olive oil
12 oz. can cola beverage
1 package dry onion soup mix
12 oz. bottle chili sauce

## Directions

Preheat oven to 325 degrees. In a small bowl, combine the cola beverage, onion soup mix, and chili sauce. Heat olive oil in Dutch oven. Sear meat on both sides until lightly browned. Place meat fat side-up. Pour cola mixture over brisket. Cover and bake for 3 hours. Uncover and cook for 1 hour more until meat is fork tender.

Transfer brisket to cutting board. Cover with foil and let rest for 15 minutes. Spoon any pan juices into gravy boat. Slice meat and serve warm with pan juices on the side.

# BRISKET WITH CRANBERRIES AND MOLASSES

*I'm a fan of molasses, so any recipes that call for this ingredient get my immediate attention. I like this variation on a brisket recipe with the fresh cranberries and pearl onions.*

## Ingredients

3 pounds flat cut beef brisket
2 Tbsp. olive oil
14.5 oz. can low sodium chicken broth
3 Tbsp. all-purpose flour
1 cup dry red wine
1 bay leaf
2 Tbsp. unsulphured molasses
2 cups water
12 oz. bag fresh cranberries
1 pound bag frozen pearl onions

## Directions

Preheat oven to 350 degrees. Heat olive oil in Dutch oven. Sear meat on both sides until lightly browned. Remove to plate. Add broth to pot and scrape up browned bits with spatula. Whisk in flour, red wine, bay leaf, molasses, 2 cups water, and half the cranberries. Bring to a boil and stir.

Return brisket to pot. Cover and bake on lower rack in oven for 3 hours. Then stir in remaining cranberries and onions and cook for 30 minutes more until meat is fork tender.

Transfer brisket to cutting board. Cover with foil and let rest for 15 minutes. Remove bay leaf from pot. Spoon any pan juices into gravy boat. Slice meat and serve warm with pan juices on the side.

# BRISKET WITH DRIED PLUMS

*If you want a recipe for Hanukkah, try this one. You get a side of tzimmes out of it with the sweet potato chunks, prunes and apricots. You can still serve potato latkes on the side.*

## Ingredients

$3^1/_2$ lb. flat cut beef brisket
2 Tbsp. olive oil
2 medium onions, sliced
1 cup beef broth
$^1/_4$ cup sweet Marsala wine
3 Tbsp. balsamic vinegar
3 Tbsp. honey
$^1/_2$ tsp. ground ginger
$^1/_2$ tsp. ground cloves
$^1/_2$ tsp. cinnamon
2 lb. sweet potatoes, peeled and cut into chunks
1 cup pitted dried plums (prunes)
1 cup dried apricots

## Directions

Preheat oven to 350 degrees. Trim fat off brisket. Heat olive oil in Dutch oven. Sear meat on both sides until lightly browned. Remove brisket and set aside. Add onions and sauté until wilted, about 5 minutes. Meanwhile, mix beef broth, Marsala wine, balsamic vinegar, honey, ginger, cloves, and cinnamon in a bowl. Put brisket on top of onions in pot. Pour broth mixture over meat.

Cover and cook for 3 hours. Then add sweet potato chunks. Scatter dried fruit on top. Cover and bake for $1/_2$ to 1 hour more until meat is fork tender.

Transfer brisket to cutting board. Cover with foil and let rest for 15 minutes. Remove fruit and sweet potatoes from pot into a separate bowl with slotted spoon. Ladle any pan juices into gravy boat. Slice meat and serve warm with fruit and potatoes on the side along with pan juices.

# CREOLE FRANKS

*If you like hot dogs as much as my father did, you'll enjoy this recipe. Ma said the original recipe called for sausages, but I prefer this version. It's an easy last-minute dish if you keep the ingredients in stock. You could even use one of those microwavable rice packages that heats in 90 seconds if you're in a rush.*

## Ingredients

3 Tbsp. olive oil
8 oz. container mixed chopped celery, onion, green pepper (trinity mix)
$1/4$ cup chopped fresh parsley
1 tsp. chopped garlic
2 packages Hebrew National reduced fat beef hot dogs
2 bay leaves
6 oz. can tomato paste
$3/4$ cup water
2 cups cooked rice

## Directions

Slice frankfurters into bite-size pieces and put aside. In a large pot, sauté chopped vegetables, parsley and garlic in oil until tender. Add franks and stir to blend. Add bay leaves, tomato paste and water. Simmer for several minutes until heated through. Discard bay leaves and serve over rice. Serves 4 to 6.

# HONEY BARBECUE MEATLOAF

*Another comfort food, this meatloaf is simple to prepare and makes for good leftovers. It's on Dalton's list of favorites. Pair it with macaroni and cheese or mashed potatoes or a medley of vegetables to cut the calories.*

## Ingredients

1$^1/_2$ pounds lean ground beef
$^1/_2$ cup dry bread crumbs
$^3/_4$ cup honey barbecue sauce
1 egg, beaten

## Directions

Preheat oven to 400 degrees. In a large bowl, combine ground beef, ½ cup sauce, bread crumbs, and beaten egg. Put into greased loaf pan. Spread remaining sauce on top. Bake for 1 hour. Remove from heat, cool for 5 minutes, then slice and serve.

Nancy J. Cohen

# JAMBALAYA

*Tally got this recipe when she and her late husband attended a cooking class in New Orleans. She substituted beef franks for the sausage and chicken for the shrimp. You can do the reverse if you wish. When I make this, it lasts us several days.*

**Ingredients**

2 Tbsp. oil
9 oz. package Perdue Short Cuts Original Roasted Chicken Breast
2 packages Hebrew National reduced fat beef hot dogs
(2) 8 oz. containers fresh diced onions
(2) 8 oz. containers mixed chopped celery, onion, green pepper (trinity mix)
1 Tbsp. chopped fresh basil
1 Tbsp. chopped garlic
1 large fresh tomato, diced
1 bunch green onions, chopped
3 cups low sodium chicken broth
2 cups uncooked jasmine rice
1 cup fresh parsley, chopped

**Directions**

Cut up the chicken and hot dogs into bite-sized pieces. Set aside in different bowls.

In a soup pot, sauté the franks in oil for flavor and then remove to a bowl. Next add diced onions, trinity mix, basil and garlic to pot and sauté until tender. Return franks to pot along with chicken, tomatoes and green onions. Add broth and bring to a boil. Add rice, cover, and simmer for 30 minutes or until most of the liquid is absorbed. Mix in parsley and serve hot. Serves 4 to 6.

# MOUSSAKA

*This is my favorite Greek dish, but then I love eggplant in anything. The skin of an eggplant contains nutrients but it's too thick to eat when the eggplant is large. I like to peel the skins for this dish and for Eggplant Parmesan. You'll also want to salt out the bitter juices from the seeds as directed. Traditional moussaka recipes may call for ground lamb instead of beef, but I prefer this variation.*

## Ingredients

1 large eggplant, peeled and sliced into thin rounds
2 Tbsp. olive oil
$1^1/_2$ to 2 pounds lean ground beef
1 small onion, chopped
15 oz. can tomato sauce
$3/_4$ cup dry red wine
2 Tbsp. chopped fresh parsley
1 tsp. dried oregano
$1/_4$ tsp. ground cinnamon
$1/_4$ cup unsalted butter
$1/_4$ cup all-purpose flour
2 cups low fat milk
3 eggs
1 cup grated Parmesan cheese, divided

## Directions

Preheat oven to 350 degrees. Grease a 9x13x2 inch baking dish.

Salt eggplant slices on both sides and let sweat on a plate for a half hour. Rinse and pat dry with paper towels.

Heat olive oil in skillet over medium high heat. Add ground beef and onions and stir until beef is browned, about 15 minutes. Stir in tomato sauce, wine, parsley, oregano and cinnamon. Simmer until mixture thickens, stirring occasionally, about 20 minutes. Set aside.

In a separate saucepan, melt butter over medium high heat. Add flour and stir 1 minute. Gradually add milk, whisking until smooth. Boil until thickened, stirring constantly, about 2 minutes.

Beat eggs in small bowl to blend. Whisk small amount of hot milk mixture into eggs. Gradually add egg mixture to saucepan, whisking constantly until mixture reaches a boil, then remove from heat. Stir in ½ cup grated Parmesan.

Arrange half of eggplant slices in bottom of baking pan. Spread meat mixture over. Top with remaining eggplant. Pour hot custard cheese sauce over eggplant. Sprinkle with remaining ½ cup Parmesan. Cover loosely with foil and bake for 1 hour. Uncover and continue baking until golden brown. Serves 6 to 8.

# POT ROAST

*Dalton is a fan of Worcestershire sauce, which he tends to sprinkle on any meat dish when he isn't using ketchup. I tend to toss in my secret ingredient of Marsala wine to give a dish added flavor. The combination below gives the meat a savory taste.*

## Ingredients

3 to 4 pound flat cut brisket
2 Tbsp. olive oil
1 large yellow onion, sliced
10.5 oz. can cream of mushroom soup
$1/2$ cup water
$3/4$ cup brown sugar
$1/4$ cup vinegar
1 tsp. Worcestershire sauce
1 tsp. mustard
$1/4$ cup sweet Marsala wine

## Directions

Heat olive oil in Dutch oven. Sear meat on both sides until lightly browned. Add sliced onions. Blend together other ingredients in a bowl and pour over meat. Cover and simmer for 2½ to 3 hours or until meat is very tender. Add water to moisten pot as needed during the cooking process.

Remove from heat, uncover, and cool slightly. Transfer meat to cutting board. Spoon any pan juices into gravy boat. Slice meat and serve warm with pan juices on the side.

# SHEPHERD'S PIE

*This comfort dish is wonderful on a chilly evening or on any night when you want a hearty meal. It provides ready-made leftovers if it's just two of you at the dinner table, and this food reheats well. It almost tastes better the next day when the flavors have blended. If you have gravy left over from another dish, you can substitute that liquid for the jar of gravy.*

## Ingredients

2 lb. prepared garlic mashed potatoes
8 oz. sliced mushrooms
2 Tbsp. olive oil
1 to 1$^1/_2$ lb. lean ground beef
1 medium onion, chopped
1 Tbsp. chopped garlic
2 Tbsp. flour
12 oz. can Heinz fat free beef gravy
$^1/_4$ cup chopped fresh parsley
$^1/_2$ tsp. dried marjoram
14.5 oz. can peas and carrots, drained
1 Tbsp. Worcestershire sauce
4 oz. shredded cheddar cheese

## Directions

Preheat oven to 350 degrees. Microwave potatoes as directed but omit adding milk or butter. In heavy large skillet, sauté mushrooms in oil and remove when wilted. Add beef, onion, and garlic to same skillet and cook on medium high heat until beef is browned. Sprinkle flour over mixture and stir. Add mushrooms, gravy, parsley, marjoram, peas and carrots, and Worcestershire sauce.

Simmer until heated through. Transfer beef mixture into a greased 9-inch square baking dish. Spoon mashed potatoes over beef layer. Sprinkle with cheddar cheese. Bake for 15 minutes or until bubbly. Serves 4 to 6.

# SLOW COOKER MUSHROOM POT ROAST

*This is an easy dish to prepare in the morning and have ready at dinner time. Serve with your favorite starch or a couple of vegetables on the side. As a hearty eater, Dalton likes any dish with meat as the main ingredient.*

## Ingredients

3 to 4 pound boneless lean beef chuck roast
2 Tbsp. canola oil
16 oz. sliced mushrooms
1 large onion, sliced
8 oz. diced celery, carrots, onion mixture
10 garlic cloves, peeled and quartered
$1^1/_2$ cups beef broth
8 oz. can tomato sauce
1 cup Burgundy wine
2 bay leaves
1 tsp. dried thyme
$^1/_4$ cup cornstarch
$^1/_4$ cup water

## Directions

Heat oil in large skillet. Sear meat on both sides until lightly browned. Put beef into slow cooker. Add the rest of the ingredients. Cook on low for 8 hours.

Transfer meat to cutting board, cover with foil, and let rest for 15 minutes. Skim fat from pan juices. Strain juices into a separate pot. Dissolve ¼ cup cornstarch into equal amount of water and stir into gravy. Cook until thickened. Pour into gravy boat. Slice meat and serve warm with gravy on the side.

89

# SPAGHETTI PIE

*I ate this at a friend's house and loved it, so I asked for the recipe. I much prefer this variation instead of spaghetti and meatballs. It's an enticing company dish when served in an attractive pie plate. This also works well reheated as leftovers.*

## Ingredients

8 oz. spaghetti
2 Tbsp. butter
2 eggs, beaten
$1/_3$ cup grated Parmesan cheese
8 oz. low fat cottage cheese
1 lb. lean ground beef
$1/_2$ cup chopped onion
14.5 oz. can petite diced tomatoes, undrained
6 oz. can tomato paste
1 tsp. sugar
1 tsp. oregano
$1/_2$ tsp. garlic powder
4 oz. shredded mozzarella cheese

## Directions

Preheat oven to 350 degrees. Cook and drain spaghetti according to package directions. Stir butter into hot spaghetti. Mix in beaten eggs and Parmesan cheese and stir until cheese is melted. Press spaghetti mixture into greased ten-inch pie plate. Spread cottage cheese over spaghetti mixture.

Meanwhile, in hot skillet, cook meat and onions until browned. Stir in tomatoes with juice, tomato paste, sugar, oregano, and garlic powder. Put meat mixture on top of cottage cheese in pie dish. Bake uncovered for twenty minutes. Sprinkle mozzarella cheese on top and bake until melted. Serves 6.

# SWEDISH MEATBALLS

*This was my grandmother's recipe, and I adore it either for a meal or for a party appetizer. If served for dinner, add cooked white rice as an accompaniment. I must confess that I've cheated and used use store-bought turkey meatballs when I'm in a hurry. If you make your own, you can assemble them in the morning, lay out the uncooked meatballs on a platter, cover and refrigerate them until later. Then make the sauce as directed, toss in the meatballs, and simmer for an hour.*

*When forming the meat mixture into balls for this recipe and the one that follows, using a small ice cream scoop or cookie scoop helps you get the right amount to pat into a ball.*

## Ingredients

$1^1/_2$ lb. lean ground beef
1 egg, beaten
$^1/_4$ tsp. garlic powder
1 cup finely chopped onions, divided
$^1/_4$ cup dry bread crumbs
12 oz. bottle chili sauce
18 oz. jar grape jelly
15 oz. can tomato sauce
$^1/_4$ cup sweet Marsala wine

## Directions

Make meatballs: Mix ground beef with beaten egg, garlic powder, ½ cup chopped onions, and bread crumbs. Form into small balls. Set aside. (Or use frozen turkey meatballs instead of making them from scratch).

In a large saucepan over medium-high heat, blend together chili sauce, grape jelly, and tomato sauce until jelly is melted. Toss in remaining onions and add wine. When mixture is bubbly, add meatballs to pot. Stir gently to coat with sauce.

Cover and reduce heat to simmer. Periodically lift lid, being careful of steam, and stir. Cook for 1 hour on low heat (or ½ hour if using frozen meatballs). Serve over cooked rice as an entrée or by itself as a party appetizer. Note: If you have extra sauce, freeze it and use as gravy in the Shepherd's Pie recipe.

# VEAL MEATBALLS WITH MUSHROOM CREAM SAUCE

*This mouth-watering entrée makes a nice presentation for a dinner party. If you're not fond of spaetzle, serve with cooked noodles or your favorite side dish. One of my mother's friends once brought this for a pot-luck dinner, and I had to try making it for myself. The creamy mushroom sauce gives it a savory flavor.*

## Ingredients

10.5 oz. box spaetzle
1 pound each of ground veal and ground turkey
$1/_2$ cup plain breadcrumbs or cornflake crumbs
2 eggs or egg substitute equivalent
2 Tbsp. dried onion flakes
1 tsp. dried thyme
2 Tbsp. butter
3 Tbsp. flour
2 cups low fat beef broth
6 oz. fresh sliced mushrooms
$1/_2$ cup chopped fresh parsley
$2/_3$ cup plain nonfat yogurt
1 Tbsp. Dijon mustard

## Directions

Prepare spaetzle according to directions on box. Drain and keep warm. Mix next five ingredients and form into small meatballs. Lay out on greased cookie sheet and bake at 350 degrees for 30 minutes.

In a nonstick skillet or electric frypan, melt butter and stir in flour. After blending, whisk in broth and cook on low heat until thickened. Add meatballs, mushrooms and parsley and stir gently. Cover and simmer until meatballs are cooked through, adding more beef broth if necessary, about 20 more minutes. Then stir in yogurt and mustard. Serve meatballs over cooked spaetzle.

# HANGING BY A HAIR

## Bad Hair Day Mystery #11

**The Recipes**
   Brisket with Dried Plums
   Chicken Spaghetti
   Israeli Couscous with Mushrooms
   Pot Roast
   Salmon Croquettes

**The Story**
   Marla's joyous move to a new house with her husband, Detective Dalton Vail, is marred by their next-door neighbor who erects an illegal fence between their properties. When Dalton reminds the man of the local permitting laws, tempers flare—and worse, the neighbor is found dead the following day. Dismayed when Dalton is removed from the case due to a conflict of interest, Marla decides it's up to her to find the killer. Can the intrepid hairstylist untangle the clues and pin down the culprit before he strikes again?

**Excerpt from Hanging by a Hair**

   As soon as Marla returned home from her errands, she made a quick call to the animal hospital to check on Spooks's status. Satisfied that her poodle was stable, she took Lucky out before putting the brisket in the Dutch oven to simmer and settling down at her computer. She wanted to look up Cherry Hunter's phone number. She accessed the homeowners' association website and found the page listing their officers.
   Marla would rather not email Cherry and risk leaving evidence of a message, so she dialed the woman's house phone instead. No one answered. She'd have to try again later.

Later never came. She got caught up on chores, confirming plans with Dalton's parents for dinner later that week, and answering her own email. A call to Luis told her to come in tomorrow morning at nine o'clock for her first appointment. Before she realized how many hours had passed, Brianna breezed in the door, home from school.

It wasn't until the next day that Marla was able to pursue Krabber's case. She wanted more than anything to help Dalton. He'd been morose the entire evening. All through her early appointments she kept wondering what else she could do.

During a break at lunch, she phoned the vet. Spooks was fine and she could pick him up after work. The bill would make her checking account considerably lighter.

Luis summoned her for a two o'clock—someone new from the unfamiliar name.

"Marla, this is Susan Feinberg," the receptionist said with his sexy grin. "She has one of your discount coupons and wants a cut and blow."

"Hi, I live in Royal Oaks and thought I'd give your salon a try." The brunette took a seat in Marla's chair. She looked to be in her thirties and had a smattering of freckles across her nose.

"I see you have highlights." Marla ruffled the lady's hair. "Are you happy with this shade?" In her opinion, the strands were too light. They should have been more subtle.

Susan made a face in the mirror. "They're too streaky, the main reason why I've wanted to change stylists. I think they left the bleach on too long."

"I can fix that for you if you wish."

"Could you tone it down? I thought I'd have to wait until my roots started to show."

"No, we can take care of it." Marla signaled to Luis and had him check the schedule to see if she'd have time. It would be a squeeze, but she could manage. "Did you say you live in Royal Oaks?" Marla said after mixing up bowls of solution and returning to her station.

"Yes, I'm in the house two doors down from yours, on the other side of Alan Krabber."

"Is that right?" She selected a comb. "His death was a horrible tragedy."

"I'll say." Susan's glance met hers in the mirror. "Who'd have thought the man would take his own life? I mean, he wasn't easy to get along with, as you well know, but still—"

"It's hard to believe," Marla finished. She picked up a foil, separated a strand of hair onto it, and painted on one of the solutions with her favorite brush. Her fingers folded the foil automatically. "Did you attend the annual meeting?"

"No, I couldn't. My husband David had to work late, so I was home watching the kids."

"How many children do you have?"

"We have a boy who's eight and a girl who's five. We moved in last June."

"I gather Alan was one of the original residents in the neighborhood."

"That's true. We didn't see much of him. He mostly kept to himself."

"Do you work outside the home?" Marla lifted another strand.

"I'm a consulting editor for a women's magazine, and I write a blog in my spare time, but I do them from my home office. It keeps my mind active." She winked at Marla in the mirror.

"I'll say. So tell me, did you have any problems with Alan?"

"Huh, who didn't? He used to complain about our kids all the time. They were too noisy, or they ran into his yard. I didn't like it when that tractor came to dig up his ground."

Susan seemed eager to talk, so Marla probed deeper. "Why do you think he wanted a big generator like that? I can understand families with young children needing power or old people who can't tolerate the heat without air conditioning, but the man seemed fairly healthy."

"Alan was more concerned with his computers than his a/c. On bulk trash day, he'd throw out lots of boxes from electronics purchases."

"I gather he was retired. Maybe that was his hobby."

"Computers? It's possible. He didn't strike me as the gamer type, though. He could have been active on the social nets." Susan gave a wicked grin. "Or maybe he played online poker."

"Now, that's a thought. One of my elderly customers loves to play online sweeps. She's actually won some prizes, too." Marla finished applying the solution. Her job done, she put down her brush and set the woman's timer.

Susan twirled in the chair to face Marla. "I heard about your debacle with the fence. It didn't surprise me. Alan was strict to enforce the rules for others but not for himself."

Marla stacked the remaining foils in a roundabout drawer. "Can you think of anyone who might have had a grudge against him?"

"Besides you and me, you mean?" Susan chortled, but then her expression turned serious. "Are you suggesting it wasn't suicide?"

"Not at all, but you never know. He didn't seem despondent to me. Who's his next of kin?" Marla asked as though she didn't possess that knowledge.

"His nephew inherits the estate, I imagine. Alan didn't have anybody else. I felt sorry for him, until I came home from grocery shopping one day and found all our patio furniture in the pool. He'd complained about our kids screaming outside his window the day before, so I'm sure it must have been him. He didn't like children or pets."

Marla wouldn't put it past Krabber, not if he was the one who'd left the bag of dog poop on their driveway. He had a mean streak that he'd kept hidden. How many other people had he offended?

**ORDER NOW** at

https://nancyjcohen.com/hanging-by-a-hair/

# ENTREES — LAMB

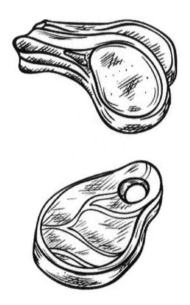

# MINTED ROAST LAMB

*My mother made this delicious recipe for Passover dinner one year. It was a big hit, and I asked for the directions. It's easy to make on a Sunday morning when you're spending time at home. I ran out of Vandermint, so I used ²/₃ cup Vandermint and ¹/₃ cup Sabra chocolate orange liqueur. This is an example of how you can make your own creative substitutions in the kitchen.*

## Ingredients

5 lb. boneless leg of lamb
¹/₂ cup water
1 cup Vandermint liqueur
¹/₂ cup butter, melted
2 Tbsp. lime juice
0.75 oz. package fresh basil, trimmed and chopped
¹/₂ cup dry white wine

## Directions

Remove lamb from refrigerator one hour before cooking to bring to room temperature. Preheat oven to 325 degrees. Place lamb on rack in roasting pan. Pour water into bottom of pan. Roast uncovered for 1 hour. In a bowl, combine Vandermint liqueur, melted butter, lime juice, and chopped basil. Baste lamb with mixture. Roast for 1½ hour more, basting occasionally. Meat thermometer should register 135 to 155 degrees, depending on how well done you like the meat.

Transfer lamb to cutting board. Cover with foil and let rest for 15 minutes before slicing. Meanwhile, skim fat from pan juices. Add remaining basting liquid and ½ cup white wine. Bring to a boil, reduce heat, and simmer for 10 minutes. Pour into gravy boat. Serve on the side with lamb. Makes 8 servings.

# SLOW COOKER ROAST LEG OF LAMB

*This makes a wonderful holiday entrée, especially in the spring. It'll suit your Easter or Passover table or be a hearty main dish for company at any other time. Using the slow cooker guarantees an extra tender meat. My grandmother served lamb with mint jelly. I like this condiment, but Dalton shakes his head at the offer. He'll reach for the Worcestershire sauce instead.*

## Ingredients

3 to 4 lb. boneless leg of lamb
4 peeled cloves garlic, cut in half
0.75 oz. package fresh rosemary
Olive oil
1 lemon, halved
1 jar mint jelly (optional)

## Directions

Using a small knife, make several incisions in the lamb. Stuff a half clove of garlic and a few rosemary sprigs into each cut. Drizzle a small amount of olive oil over lamb. Place the meat in the slow cooker. Squeeze the lemon over the lamb, and drop the lemon shells into the slow cooker. Cook the lamb on low for 8 hours or until the meat easily pulls apart. It should register at least 135 degrees on a meat thermometer.

Uncover and discard lemon shells and rosemary sprigs. Transfer meat to cutting board. Cover with foil and let rest for 15 minutes. Slice and serve warm with mint jelly on the side. Serves 6 to 8.

# LAMB RAGOUT

*This is a super easy dish to make from leftover lamb (see roast leg of lamb above). It'll make enough for several days so you can benefit for the rest of the week.*

## Ingredients

8 oz. container mixed chopped celery, onion, green pepper (trinity mix)
8 oz. chopped green onions
2 Tbsp. olive oil
1 to 2 cups shredded roast lamb
4 oz. jar diced pimento, drained
8 oz. can diced water chestnuts, drained
12 oz. jar mushroom gravy
$1/_2$ tsp. curry powder
$1/_2$ tsp. paprika
$1/_4$ tsp. oregano
6 oz. can fried onions, divided
$1/_2$ cup slivered almonds

## Directions

Preheat oven to 350 degrees. Heat olive oil in large pot. Sauté trinity mix and green onions until vegetables are wilted. Mix in shredded roast lamb, pimento, water chestnuts, gravy, seasonings, and ¼ can fried onions. Put mixture into greased 9x13x2 inch baking dish. Sprinkle the rest of the fried onions and the slivered almonds on top.

Bake until sides are bubbly and food is heated through, about 20 minutes. Serves 4 to 6.

# EASTER HAIR HUNT

## Bad Hair Day Mystery #16

### The Recipes
Slow Cooker Roast Leg of Lamb
Roasted Acorn Squash
Rosemary Red Potatoes
Garlic Cheese Biscuits
Slow Cooker Mushroom Pot Roast
Tilapia Dijon

### The Story
Hairstylist Marla Vail attends an Easter Egg Hunt that takes place at historic Tremayne Manor. Her friend Blinky is playing the Easter bunny. Blinky, a client at Marla's salon, has hired Marla to fix her hair afterwards for a charity luncheon at the mansion. But once the children's event is over, Marla can't find Blinky anywhere. As she's searching the grounds, she stumbles across a costumed figure sprawled on the lawn. The person is still as a dead hare. Afraid Blinky has fainted in the stuffy costume, Marla summons help. But when rescuers pull off the face mask, shock ripples through her. A dead stranger has taken her friend's place. When it turns out to be a case of murder, Marla fears for Blinky's safety. Can she use her eggcellent sleuthing skills to hunt down her friend before Blinky becomes the next victim?

### Excerpt from Easter Hair Hunt

As Sunday rolled around, Marla's prediction came true. Dalton left early to go into his office. Marla got started preparing the leg of lamb to put into the slow cooker. Kate—Dalton's mom—had bought the pot for her as a holiday gift.

She said Marla would be super busy once the baby arrived, and putting in a meal to simmer all day might be helpful.

As per the recipe she'd found, Marla cut slits into the meat and inserted sprigs of rosemary and garlic cloves into these strategic locations. After drizzling olive oil over the roast, she placed it into the slow cooker. Next she squeezed cut halves of lemon over the top and dropped the shells into the pot. With the temperature on low, she set the timer for eight hours.

She considered what to do next. A spinach salad would start off the main meal. That was Dalton's domain. He'd put all the ingredients together when he got home. Rosemary red potatoes and fresh asparagus were the accompaniments, but she wouldn't prepare those until later.

She'd come across a recipe online for acorn squash slices and had asked Dalton to bring home some squashes so she could try it. The recipe used herbs, not brown sugar or maple syrup, so it should be healthier with less calories. She figured they couldn't have enough side dishes, and this occasion gave her the excuse to try something new.

Ma was bringing a carrot cake for dessert, and Kate and John were bringing wine. Brianna had called dibs on making garlic cheese biscuits.

Soon the house filled with delicious aromas. Brianna, after segregating the ingredients she would use later, went to her room to finish her homework. Marla assembled the stuffed mushrooms and chili dip she'd serve for appetizers and refrigerated them to bake later.

Tired of working in the kitchen, she took the dogs for a walk to get some fresh air. The day had turned out temperate and sunny. She said hello to Susan Feinberg a couple of doors down. Susan, a friend and neighbor as well as a client at Marla's salon, was the same age as Marla. She had two school-age children and baked the best brownies on the block.

"You look nice," Susan commented while her kids fumbled over a basketball. Her son won the skirmish with his younger sister and tossed the ball into a portable weighted net. "Are you going out for a holiday dinner today?"

"Our families are coming over," Marla explained. "I just did my hair and makeup. I'll change into something nicer later." Susan already knew that while Marla was Jewish, Dalton was not. They'd made the decision early in their two-year-old marriage to respect both religions.

"How many people are you having?" Susan inquired.

"Dalton's parents are coming, along with my mother and her boyfriend. We're also expecting my brother and his family, which will be nice since we haven't seen each other in a while. That makes eleven of us altogether." *Twelve, if you count the baby growing inside me.*

Marla rubbed her belly, feeling a kick in response. She smiled inwardly, her heart swelling with love for the child joined to her. It was still difficult to conceive that she and Dalton were expecting a baby. Marla hadn't wanted kids of her own until recently, and now at thirty-nine, she hoped there wouldn't be any complications.

"We should go to lunch," Susan suggested. "I see you at the salon when you do my hair and around the neighborhood, but we haven't had a good schmooze in some time."

"I know, and I could use your advice. Dalton wants to buy baby furniture, but I'm afraid to tempt fate. Things could still happen, if you know what I mean."

Susan gave her a bemused glance. "Things can always happen, Marla. You can't think that way. It's fun to go shopping to furnish your nursery. Better now than later, when you'll have a hundred other things to do. Call me this week, and we'll set a date to get together."

The dogs strained on their leash as Marla strode along the sidewalk. Her stomach churned as she mused over the changes in her life about to occur. Hopefully, Dalton's parents wouldn't pressure her about baby shopping. She got enough on that topic from Ma. Maybe she could steer the conversation to their latest case rather than to her personal issues. Ma's boyfriend, Reed, got a kick out of her sleuthing. The former literature professor enjoyed a challenge.

Speaking of challenges, she gave Dalton one in the kitchen that afternoon. He'd come home from work with the acorn squashes she'd requested. Occupied with retrieving serving platters, Marla asked him to stick a squash in the microwave for five minutes. Once softened, she could slice it and save the baking part for later.

She'd lined up her serving dishes and was drying dishes by the sink when a loud popping noise sounded from behind. She whipped around just as the microwave door burst open. With a shriek, she leapt back. That thing might have cracked her on the head if she'd stood in front of it.

Regaining her equilibrium, she dropped her dish towel and went over to cancel the programming. Oh no. Dalton had timed it for fifteen minutes, not five minutes as requested! Her pulse still raced as she regarded the mangled mess inside the oven. Steam billowed from the interior.

"You should have pricked the skin if you put it in for that long," she admonished Dalton, who'd rushed over from his perch in front of the TV. He gaped at the microwave unit, his astonished expression diminishing her annoyance.

"What do you mean?"

"I told you to put it in for five minutes, not fifteen. Pricking the skin lets air escape so the squash doesn't explode. It's a good thing we have more of them to cook."

His forehead creased. "Thank goodness you weren't hurt. That's all that matters."

Brianna wandered into the room. "What did you do, Dad?"

He pointed to his chest. "Hey, why does everybody blame me? How am I supposed to know about these things? If you want it done right, do it yourself."

"It's okay, hon." Marla sidled closer and kissed him. "I'll

clean it up, and no one will be the wiser. That is, if the microwave isn't broken."

The only thing broken was Dalton's pride. He slinked off to the family room to watch TV, while Brianna and Marla discussed baking times for their respective dishes and the order for oven usage. Coordinating a holiday meal took advance planning.

****

For more details, go to
https://nancyjcohen.com/easter-hair-hunt/

# ENTREES — POULTRY

# CHICKEN ASPARAGUS

*This is a quick dish to prepare and an all-in-one meal with protein and vegetables. It's a good dinner to make after work when you don't feel like spending much time in the kitchen.*

## Ingredients

1 pound fresh asparagus, trimmed
2 Tbsp. olive oil
1 red bell pepper, seeded and sliced thin
(2) 9 oz. packages Perdue roasted carved chicken breast
1 cup whipping cream
3.5 oz. jar pesto sauce

## Directions

Place asparagus in microwave-safe dish, add 2 Tbsp. water, cover and cook on high for two minutes. Remove to plate and cut into bite-size pieces. Meanwhile, heat oil in large skillet. Sauté red bell pepper and asparagus until crisp-tender. Stir in cooked chicken. Add whipping cream and pesto sauce, mix to blend and heat through. Serve over rice or cooked couscous. Note: You can substitute leftover chicken or turkey from another dish for these packaged cuts. Makes 4 to 6 servings.

# CHICKEN BASQUE

*I'm fond of the darker cuts of chicken, so anything with boneless thighs gets my interest. This dish comes out tender and includes potatoes, so you don't need much else to go with it except for a salad.*

## Ingredients

$1^1/_2$ pounds boneless, skinless chicken thighs, cut into 2 inch chunks
2 Tbsp. olive oil
1 onion, sliced
1 red bell pepper, cut into strips
2 cloves garlic, minced
14.5 oz. can diced tomatoes, drained
1 lb. red potatoes cut into bite-size chunks
14.5 oz. can chicken broth
$1/_4$ tsp. each dried thyme and dried savory
4 oz. jar diced pimento, drained

## Directions

In a Dutch oven, heat oil over medium heat. Add chicken and brown on all sides. Add onion and red bell pepper. Cook until slightly wilted. Add garlic and stir. Add the remaining ingredients. Cover and simmer for 30 minutes or until chicken and potatoes are tender. Serves 4 to 6.

# CHICKEN BEAN STEW

*Dalton loves this dish that's a hearty but healthy stew with chicken and cannellini beans. It's a tasty meal-in-one and makes enough for leftovers, if there's only two of you or if you cut the breast pieces in half per portion size.*

## Ingredients

5 to 6 boneless, skinless chicken breasts
$1/_3$ cup all-purpose flour
3 Tbsp. olive oil
1 medium onion, cut into chunks
8 oz. fresh sliced carrots
1 tsp. chopped garlic
14.5 oz. can diced tomatoes with juice
14.5 oz. can low sodium chicken broth
$1/_4$ cup dry red wine (or more if needed to moisturize)
15 oz. can low sodium cannellini beans, drained and rinsed

## Directions

Preheat oven to 350 degrees. Sprinkle flour on a plate and dredge chicken pieces to coat. Heat 2 Tbsp. oil in a Dutch oven and brown chicken on all sides. Remove from pot. Deglaze with a bit of broth and add 1 Tbsp. oil. Stir in onion and carrots and sauté until onions wilt. Add garlic and stir. Add diced tomatoes. Place chicken on top. Pour broth and red wine over chicken.

Bring to a boil. Turn off burner, cover pot, and cook in oven for 30 minutes. Add beans. Cook for 30 minutes more or until chicken is done. Serves 4 to 6.

# CHICKEN BROCCOLI CASSEROLE

*My mother created this dish by altering a magazine recipe and adding curry powder that she'd bought on a cruise to Grenada. There's an extra step in preparing the rice first, but you can always use leftover rice if available or one of those microwavable packets. If it's just Dalton and me eating, and we have too much rice left at a previous meal, I'll freeze a container and use it later in a casserole like this one.*

## Ingredients

6 to 8 oz. package long grain and wild rice mix
16 oz. package frozen broccoli florets, defrosted
9 oz. package Perdue short cuts original roasted chicken breast
$1/_2$ cup shredded cheddar cheese
1 cup sliced mushrooms
4 oz. jar diced pimento, drained
10.5 oz. can cream of mushroom soup
1 cup plain yogurt
$1/_3$ cup mayonnaise
1 tsp. mustard
$1/_4$ tsp. curry powder
2 Tbsp. grated Parmesan cheese

## Directions

Preheat oven to 350 degrees. Spray a 9x13x2 inch baking dish with cooking spray. Prepare rice according to package directions, omitting butter. Layer rice, broccoli, chicken, cheddar cheese, mushrooms, and pimento in greased baking pan.

In a small bowl, combine soup, yogurt, mayonnaise, mustard, and curry powder. Spread evenly over top of casserole. Sprinkle with Parmesan cheese. Bake uncovered for 40 minutes or until heated through. Serves 6 to 8.

# CHICKEN CACCIATORE

*This classic dish is always a crowd-pleaser. Add your own variation if you have some chopped parsley on hand or another vegetable in stock that you want to use.*

## Ingredients

5 to 6 boneless, skinless chicken breasts
2 Tbsp. olive oil
1 onion, chopped
1 green bell pepper, seeded and chopped
16 oz. fresh mushrooms, sliced
1 Tbsp. minced garlic
1 tsp. dried basil
1 tsp. dried oregano
1 cup dry red wine
28 oz. can diced tomatoes

## Directions

In a large skillet, sauté the chicken breasts in olive oil until browned on both sides. Remove to a plate and set aside. Add onion and bell pepper to pan and cook until soft, about 5 minutes. Add mushrooms and garlic and stir occasionally until mushrooms are tender. Sprinkle on basil and oregano. Pour in the red wine and bring to a boil.

Cook until wine is reduced by half, about 5 minutes. Stir in the tomatoes and add the chicken to the mixture. Cover and reduce heat to a simmer. Cook for 30 to 45 minutes or until chicken is done. Serve over cooked noodles or rice. Makes 4 to 6 servings.

Nancy J. Cohen

# CHICKEN CRANBERRY

*As you might guess, this dish is great to make in the fall when fresh cranberries are in season. They'll add a splash of color to your chicken dish and make an ordinary meal seem festive.*

**Ingredients**

$1^1/_2$ pounds boneless, skinless chicken thighs
2 Tbsp. olive oil
3 shallots, peeled and chopped
8 oz. bag fresh cranberries, rinsed
$^3/_4$ cup water
$^1/_3$ cup apple cider vinegar
1 Tbsp. honey
$^3/_4$ tsp. ground ginger
$^1/_4$ tsp. allspice

**Directions**

Preheat oven to 400 degrees. Heat olive oil in large skillet. Sauté shallots until beginning to brown. Add cranberries, water, vinegar and honey. Cook until the berries soften and begin to burst, stirring occasionally. When cranberries are softened, add the ginger and allspice.

Place chicken thighs in greased 9x13x2 inch baking dish. Spread cranberry mixture over chicken. Bake for 30 to 45 minutes or until chicken is done. Serves 4 to 6.

# CHICKEN DIVINE

*This company dish lives up to its name and is simple to prepare. You can decrease the cooking time if you use boneless, skinless breasts instead of bone-in ones.*

## Ingredients

6 bone-in chicken breasts
16 oz. sliced mushrooms
3 green onions, chopped
1 tsp. dried rosemary
Juice from 1 lemon
1 Tbsp. chopped garlic
2 Tbsp. chopped fresh parsley
$1/_2$ cup dry white wine
$1/_2$ cup chicken broth
1 Tbsp. flour mixed in 3 Tbsp. water

## Directions

Preheat oven to 400 degrees. Spread mushrooms in bottom of greased 9x13x2 inch baking pan. Sprinkle with green onions. Place chicken breasts on top. Cover with rosemary, lemon juice, garlic, and parsley. Pour the white wine and chicken broth over all. Cover and bake for 40 minutes.

Remove cover and bake until chicken is cooked through and browned, about 20 minutes more. Remove dish from oven and plate chicken. Keep warm. Meanwhile, make gravy. Add pan juices into measuring cup with enough water added to make 2 cups. Add sauce to pot and whisk in flour mixture. Heat to a simmer and stir until thickened. Serve with chicken. Serves 6.

# CHICKEN EGGPLANT

*This can be another one-dish wonder served along with a salad. You get your vegetable and protein all in one tasty ensemble. If you're an eggplant lover, this meal is for you.*

## Ingredients

1 medium eggplant, peeled and cut into 1 inch cubes
Salt
24 oz. jar tomato basil sauce
5 to 6 boneless, skinless chicken breasts
6 oz. shredded mozzarella cheese
$1/4$ cup chopped fresh basil

## Directions

Preheat oven to 350 degrees. Place eggplant chunks in colander over sink and sprinkle with salt. Let stand for 30 minutes. Rinse bitter juice away and pat dry with a paper towel. Add eggplant to a large bowl and mix in tomato basil sauce. Meanwhile, in a large nonstick skillet coated with cooking spray, brown chicken breasts on both sides.

Place chicken in greased 9x13x2 inch baking dish. Sprinkle with half the mozzarella cheese. Top with eggplant mixture and then remaining cheese. Sprinkle chopped basil on top. Cover and bake for 40 minutes or until chicken is cooked through. Serves 4 to 6.

# CHICKEN MAC AND CHEESE

*Easy to prepare, this meal is comfort food at its best, combining flaked chicken with mac and cheese. The peas and pimento add color, and the fried onions contribute lip-smacking flavor. You'll want seconds on this dish.*

## Ingredients

12 oz. box macaroni and cheese mix
12 oz. can chunk chicken breast, drained
10.5 oz. can cream of mushroom soup
$1\frac{1}{3}$ cups 2% milk
9 oz. package frozen peas and pearl onions, thawed
4 oz. jar diced pimento, drained
8 oz. sliced mushrooms
6 oz. can fried onions

## Directions

Preheat oven to 325 degrees. Prepare macaroni and cheese dinner according to directions. Pour into large bowl. Mix in the chicken, soup, milk, peas and onions, pimento, mushrooms, and half of the fried onions. Put mixture into a greased 2 quart baking dish and cook in oven for 25 to 30 minutes. Sprinkle with remaining fried onions and bake until browned and bubbly. Serves 4 to 6.

# CHICKEN ORZO

*This is another easy dish and one-pot meal. Add a salad or extra vegetable on the side, and you'll have all you need.*

## Ingredients

1 cup uncooked orzo pasta
2 Tbsp. olive oil
2 tsp. chopped garlic
1 package Perdue short cuts cooked chicken breast, cut into bite-size pieces
(2) 14.5 oz. cans stewed tomatoes, cut up
15 oz. can low sodium cannellini beans, drained and rinsed
16 oz. package frozen broccoli florets, thawed
1 tsp. Italian seasoning

## Directions

Cook pasta according to directions on box. Drain and put aside. In a separate large skillet, sauté garlic in oil until tender. Stir in chicken, tomatoes, beans, broccoli, and Italian seasoning. Mix in pasta. Heat until warmed through. Serves 4 to 6.

# CHICKEN PAPRIKA

*This makes a nice company dish that you can serve with rice or another side of your choice. The barley recipes listed below under side dishes would be a good accompaniment.*

## Ingredients

$1/_4$ cup butter
3 Tbsp. all-purpose flour
2 Tbsp. paprika
1 tsp. poultry seasoning
8 boneless, skinless chicken thighs
10.5 oz. can cream of mushroom soup
1 cup reduced fat milk
8 oz. fresh sliced mushrooms
2 Tbsp. chopped fresh parsley
$1/_4$ tsp. dried thyme

## Directions

Preheat oven to 350 degrees. Melt butter in microwave. Remove from oven and stir in flour, paprika, and poultry seasoning. Place chicken in greased 9x13x2 inch baking dish. Spread buttery paprika mixture over chicken. In a separate bowl, whisk the soup and milk until blended. Stir in sliced mushrooms. Pour liquid mixture over chicken. Sprinkle parsley and thyme on top.

Bake covered for 35 minutes. Uncover and bake for 20 minutes more or until chicken is cooked through. Serves 4.

# CHICKEN RASPBERRY

*If you have any raspberry vinegar in your pantry, try this recipe. I made it by mistake when I'd asked Dalton to get me the bottle of balsamic vinegar, and he handed me the raspberry vinegar instead. I'd added it to the dish before noticing the label. It turned out so well that I changed the ingredient on my recipe to match.*

**Ingredients**

4 to 6 boneless, skinless chicken breasts
2 Tbsp. butter
2 Tbsp. vegetable oil
$2/_3$ cup low sodium chicken broth
3 large shallots, peeled and chopped
$1/_2$ cup raspberry vinegar
$1/_2$ tsp. dried rosemary
$2/_3$ cup heavy whipping cream

**Directions**

Preheat oven to 350 degrees. In a Dutch oven, heat the butter and oil until melted. Brown chicken breasts on both sides and remove from pan. Deglaze pan with chicken broth then add shallots. Bring to a simmer. Add raspberry vinegar and bring to a boil. Place chicken breasts in pot, sprinkle with rosemary, and cover.

Bake for 30 minutes. Remove pot from oven, mix in whipping cream, and flip breasts over onto other side. Bake uncovered for 15 minutes more. Serves 4 to 6.

# CHICKEN SPAGHETTI

*This is my favorite one-dish meal to make for a sick friend or one that will stretch for a few nights. Keep the ingredients in stock for when you need a last-minute dinner. You may substitute canned white meat chicken for the short cuts, frozen mixed vegetables or canned peas and carrots for the vegetable portion, and cream of mushroom or celery for the soup. You can also use any shredded cheese you have on hand. As an option, add a can of drained sliced water chestnuts for extra crunch. Or sprinkle slivered almonds on top.*

## Ingredients

16 oz. box spaghetti, vermicelli, or angel hair pasta
9 oz. package Roasted Chicken Breast Short Cuts
16 oz. package frozen peas and carrots
1 cup shredded cheddar cheese, divided
(2) 10.5 oz. cans Healthy Request cream of chicken soup
4 oz. jar diced pimento, drained

## Directions

Preheat oven to 350 degrees. Grease a 9x13x2 inch baking dish. Cook pasta according to package directions. Drain and put into a large bowl. Add all other ingredients, reserving ¼ cup cheddar cheese, and mix to blend. Pour mixture into baking dish. Sprinkle remaining cheese on top. Bake until browned and bubbly, about 20 minutes. Serves 6 to 8.

# CHICKEN STEW

*This meal adds potatoes to another boneless chicken thigh recipe, so you don't need to prepare much else except perhaps another cooked vegetable or a fresh salad. This is a good winter dish that will warm you up on a chilly night.*

## Ingredients

8 boneless, skinless chicken thighs
1 lb. petite red potatoes, quartered
8 oz. fresh sliced carrots
1 large onion, cut into small chunks
14.5 oz. can low sodium chicken broth
6 oz. can tomato paste
2 Tbsp. olive oil
1 Tbsp. ground saffron
1 tsp. ground cumin

## Directions

Preheat oven to 400 degrees. Place the cut potatoes, carrots, and onion into a greased 9x13x2 inch baking dish. Place chicken on top. Combine remaining ingredients in a small bowl and pour over chicken. Cover and bake for 60 minutes or until chicken is cooked through and vegetables are tender. Serves 4 to 6.

# CHICKEN TENDERLOINS

*Dalton loves these chicken tenderloins and gobbles them up even without the sauce. They're so tasty that you will have to eat more than one or two. This goes well with just about any side dish. Try it with the Spinach Noodle Surprise for a creamy accompaniment.*

## Ingredients

1 pound chicken tenderloins
2 Tbsp. mayonnaise
2 Tbsp. prepared fresh grated white horseradish
$1/2$ cup dry bread crumbs
2 Tbsp. chopped fresh parsley

## Sauce
$1/4$ cup mayonnaise
$1/4$ cup fat free plain yogurt
1 Tbsp. prepared fresh grated white horseradish
1 Tbsp. Dijon mustard
$1/4$ tsp. paprika

## Directions

Preheat oven to 400 degrees. Combine 2 Tbsp. mayonnaise and 2 Tbsp. horseradish in a small bowl. Dip chicken in mixture and then roll in bread crumbs mixed with parsley. Place chicken tenders in greased 9-inch square baking dish and bake for 30 minutes or until chicken is cooked through. Meanwhile, combine the next five ingredients for the sauce in a small bowl and cover until meal is ready. Serve baked chicken with dipping sauce on the side. Serves 4.

Nancy J. Cohen

# CHICKEN THIGHS DIJON

*Brianna likes to make this easy recipe when she's in the mood to cook. Our stepdaughter is becoming as interested in cooking as she is in sleuthing. That is, when she has time between the debate team, her athletics, and acting classes. She'll come home from school, assemble this dish, and bake it right before we're ready to eat. A microwavable rice mixture is her side dish of choice along with a packaged salad. Today is all about convenience for many of us, but the only way to control the ingredients is to cook a meal yourself. We need to get our kids in the kitchen early to teach them these skills.*

**Ingredients**

8 boneless, skinless chicken thighs
2 Tbsp. olive oil
1 Tbsp. balsamic vinegar
1 tsp. brown sugar
1 Tbsp. Dijon mustard
4 garlic cloves, chopped

**Directions**

Preheat oven to 400 degrees. Put the chicken into a greased 9x13x2 inch baking dish. In a separate bowl, mix the olive oil with the balsamic vinegar, brown sugar, mustard, and garlic and then spread over chicken. Bake for 35 minutes, or until cooked through. Serves 4 to 6.

# CHICKEN THIGHS WITH MUSHROOMS

*This quick recipe adds mushrooms, green onions, and garlic—always flavorful additions to a meal. I can't wait until these baked chicken thighs come out of the oven when I make them. The aroma brings everyone into the kitchen along with their appetites.*

## Ingredients

6 boneless, skinless chicken thighs
2 Tbsp. spicy brown mustard
2 Tbsp. olive oil
8 oz. sliced mushrooms
2 tsp. minced garlic
2 green onions, chopped

## Directions

Preheat oven to 400 degrees. In a small bowl, mix together the mustard and olive oil. In a separate bowl, toss together mushrooms, garlic, and green onions. Place vegetables in greased 9x13x2 inch baking dish. Put chicken on top of mushroom mixture. Brush with mustard and oil blend. Bake for 35 minutes, or until cooked through. Serves 4.

# COCONUT CHICKEN CURRY

*My mother likes curry recipes. She served this to us one night, and it was an instant hit. It's a great entrée for an island-themed party or a Caribbean night dinner.*

## Ingredients

5 boneless, skinless chicken breasts
4 Tbsp. olive oil
2 Tbsp. curry powder
13.5 oz. can lite coconut milk
1 large onion, sliced
2 Tbsp. chopped garlic
8 oz. can bamboo shoots, drained
Cooked rice

## Directions

Cut chicken into bite-size pieces and refrigerate until needed. In a large skillet, heat 2 Tbsp. olive oil. Add curry powder and swirl it around until blended. Pour in the coconut milk and stir. Keep on low heat.

In a separate skillet or electric frypan, sauté the garlic and onions in the remaining olive oil. Once the onions are wilted, add the cubed chicken. Brown on all sides. Add bamboo shoots and pour in coconut milk mixture. Cover and simmer for 30 minutes. Serve over cooked rice. Makes 4 servings.

# GINGER CHICKEN THIGHS

*If you're a fan of fresh ginger, you'll like this easy recipe that doesn't take long to prepare. Note it uses my secret ingredient, a splash of Marsala wine.*

## Ingredients

1 boil-in bag brown rice
2 Tbsp. chopped green onions
6 boneless, skinless chicken thighs
2 Tbsp. olive oil
2 tsp. chopped garlic
2 tsp. chopped peeled ginger
$1/_2$ cup apricot preserves
2 Tbsp. low sodium soy sauce
2 Tbsp. sweet Marsala wine

## Directions

Cook rice as directed, drain, and then empty into serving bowl. Sprinkle green onions on top and set aside. Meanwhile, sauté chicken in oil in large skillet until browned on all sides. Remove to separate plate and keep warm. Add garlic and ginger to pan, and cook for a minute or two. Then add preserves, soy sauce, and wine. Stir to blend.

Put chicken back in pan, coat in juices, and cover. Simmer until chicken is cooked through, about 30 minutes. Serve with cooked rice. Makes 4 servings.

# HURRICANE HASH

*After one of the hurricanes that hit South Florida, I tossed together this concoction. It came from items I had in stock. Fortunately, we had power, but the roads had trees down and it wasn't safe to drive far. Feel free to use whatever ingredients you have on hand. For example, you can substitute spaghetti for the rice, parsley for the dill, add diced tomatoes, or change the recipe otherwise to suit your ingredients. Cream of celery or cream of chicken soup can be substituted for the mushroom soup.*

## Ingredients

2 cups uncooked long-grain rice
(2) 12.5 oz. cans chicken breast meat
4 oz. shredded mozzarella cheese
$1/4$ cup grated Parmesan cheese
8.5 oz. can peas and carrots
(2) 10.5 oz. cans cream of mushroom soup
2 Tbsp. chopped fresh dill

## Directions

Preheat oven to 350 degrees. Cook rice according to package directions. Flake chicken breast in large bowl. Add all other ingredients including cooked rice. If desired, add salt to taste. Spread into greased 9x13x2 inch baking dish. Bake for 30 minutes, or until heated through. Serves 4 to 6.

# ISLAND TURKEY THIGHS

*Are you unable to escape from your own bad hair days? Trade your blow-dryer and comb for a spatula and spoon, and try this recipe to lift your mood. Light a coconut-scented candle, play some Caribbean music, and imagine yourself sailing to the tropics. The Caribbean Rice with Pigeon Peas makes a tasty side dish to accompany this entrée.*

## Ingredients

8 oz. container chopped onions
8 oz. container chopped celery
8 oz. chopped carrots
$1/_3$ cup ketchup
$1/_2$ tsp. paprika
4 pounds turkey thighs
1 large size oven bag
1 Tbsp. flour
$1/_3$ cup dry white wine
$1/_2$ cup low sodium chicken broth
2 bay leaves

## Directions

Preheat oven to 350 degrees. In a bowl, combine vegetables, ketchup, and paprika. Place flour in oven bag; shake to coat. Rinse and pat dry turkey thighs, then place in bag. Put into a 9x13x2 inch baking dish. Sprinkle vegetable mixture over turkey, then pour on wine and broth. Add bay leaves and seal bag. Cut slits in top. Bake for 1-1/2 hours. Remove bay leaves before serving. Serves 6 to 8.

# LYCHEE CURRY CHICKEN

*My mother created this family favorite when she had fresh lychees from the tree in her yard. It's a colorful stir-fry dish with healthy vegetables. The lychees give it a unique taste.*

## Ingredients

1 pound chicken tenderloins
1 Tbsp. curry powder
2 tsp. powdered ginger
2 Tbsp. canola oil
1 package sugar snap peas, ends trimmed
1 red bell pepper, cut into strips
8 oz. package sliced zucchini
$1/2$ bunch green onions, chopped
$1/3$ cup reduced fat chicken broth
$1/2$ cup fresh lychees, chopped and drained, liquid reserved.
Hot cooked rice

## Directions

Trim the tendons off the chicken and cut the meat into one-inch chunks. In a bowl, mix the curry powder and ginger and toss in the chicken to coat. In a large nonstick skillet, heat the oil. Add the chicken and stir-fry until browned on all sides. Add the peas, pepper, zucchini, green onions, lychees, broth, and reserved lychee juice. Mix well, cover and simmer until vegetables are tender and chicken is cooked through. Serve over rice. Makes 4 servings.

# MUSHROOM-STUFFED CHICKEN

*This company dish will impress your friends. It's relatively easy to put together in a few steps. Serve with your side dish of choice along with a mixed salad or colorful vegetable.*

## Ingredients

4 to 6 boneless, skinless chicken breasts
$1/4$ cup chopped green onions
8 oz. sliced mushrooms
1 tsp. minced garlic
$1/2$ tsp. dried thyme
2 oz. shredded mozzarella cheese
$1/4$ cup flour
$1/4$ cup dry bread crumbs
$1/2$ cup egg substitute or 2 eggs, beaten
1 Tbsp. olive oil

## Directions

Preheat oven to 350 degrees. Grease a 9x13x2 inch baking dish.

Coat a large skillet with cooking spray. Sauté green onions, mushrooms, and garlic at medium-high heat until wilted. Stir in thyme. Remove from heat and mix in cheese. Meanwhile, cut a slit through the thickest part of each chicken breast. Stuff each breast with ¼ cup mushroom mixture.

Place flour, bread crumbs, and beaten eggs in separate plates. Dip each chicken breast in flour, egg, and bread crumbs respectively. Heat oil in skillet and brown chicken on both sides. Transfer to baking dish and bake for 30 to 45 minutes or until cooked through. Serves 4 to 6.

## QUICK TURKEY CURRY

*This is a great way to use turkey leftovers. If you want to cut the prep time, buy two 8 oz. packages of pre-chopped green peppers, celery, and onions at the grocery store as a substitute for the first three ingredients. You might find a container of sliced green onions as well. I always keep many of these ingredients in stock, so it's a matter of pulling together all the components and adding fresh vegetables.*

**Ingredients**

1 cup diced green pepper
$^{1}/_{2}$ cup diced celery
$^{1}/_{2}$ large sweet onion, diced
4 green onions, sliced
2 Tbsp. canola oil
1 to 2 cups cooked turkey breast, cut into bite-size pieces
8 oz. can sliced water chestnuts, drained
2 oz. package slivered almonds
4 Tbsp. all-purpose flour
$^{1}/_{2}$ tsp. curry powder
$^{1}/_{2}$ tsp. paprika
$^{1}/_{4}$ tsp. dried basil
16 oz. low sodium chicken broth
4 oz. jar diced pimento, drained
Cooked rice

**Directions**

In a large skillet, sauté the green pepper, celery, and onions in oil until wilted. Stir in the turkey, water chestnuts, and almonds. Meanwhile, in a small bowl, whisk the flour, curry powder, paprika and basil into the broth until blended. Stir into the skillet mixture and add pimento. Cover and simmer until heated through. Serve over rice. Makes 4 to 6 servings.

# ROAST TURKEY BREAST WITH HERBS

*If you don't feel like roasting a whole turkey, this is a good substitute for a holiday meal. It's especially useful for a smaller gathering. You'll have some carving to do but not the entire bird.*

## Ingredients

6 to 7 pound bone-in turkey breast
2 Tbsp. olive oil
1 Tbsp. minced garlic
2 tsp. fresh lemon juice
2 tsp. dry mustard
1 Tbsp. dried rosemary
1 Tbsp. dried sage
1 tsp. dried thyme
$^3/_4$ cup dry white wine

## Directions

Preheat oven to 325 degrees. Place the turkey breast in a roasting pan, skin side up. In a small bowl, combine olive oil, garlic, lemon juice, mustard, rosemary, sage and thyme. Rub over turkey. Pour the wine into the bottom of the pan. Roast uncovered for 1½ hours or longer until meat thermometer registers 165 degrees in thickest part of breast. Cover breast with foil if overbrowning occurs during cooking time.

When done, transfer turkey breast to cutting board, cover with foil, and allow to rest for 15 minutes before carving. Reserve pan juices for gravy. Serves 6 to 8.

# SLOW COOKER APRICOT CHICKEN

*This dish makes a nice presentation for company and helps use up some of that apricot brandy in your cupboard. The chicken comes out deliciously tender. If you can't find skinless, bone-in thighs, get regular chicken thighs and remove skin.*

## Ingredients

8 skinless, bone-in chicken thighs
2 Tbsp. canola oil
1 large onion, sliced
$1/4$ cup apricot brandy
$1/4$ cup honey
2 Tbsp. Dijon mustard
$1/2$ cup chicken broth
6 oz. package dried apricots, halved
Chopped fresh parsley

## Directions

Heat canola oil in large skillet. Sear chicken thighs on both sides until lightly browned. Transfer chicken to large size slow cooker. Add sliced onions to skillet and sauté until wilted. Add brandy and deglaze particles on skillet bottom. Turn off heat and add onions to slow cooker. In a separate bowl, whisk together the honey, Dijon mustard, and chicken broth. Pour over onions. Cover and cook on low for 4 hours, adding apricots halfway through cooking time. Garnish with chopped parsley before serving. Serves 4 to 6.

# SLOW COOKER TURKEY BREAST

*Cousin Cynthia finds simple ways to cook so she doesn't have to spend a lot of time in the kitchen. She gave me this recipe that's an easy way to make turkey. It's good for a family or for stashing leftovers if there are only two of you.*

## Ingredients

$3^1/_2$ to 4 pounds boneless, skinless turkey breasts
$^1/_4$ cup packed brown sugar
1 Tbsp. sage
1 Tbsp. thyme
1 Tbsp. marjoram
1 tsp. garlic powder
1 tsp. paprika
1 package dry onion soup mix
14.5 oz. can low sodium chicken broth
$^1/_2$ cup lemon juice
$^1/_4$ cup lime juice
$^1/_4$ cup cider vinegar
$^1/_4$ cup olive oil
2 tsp. Dijon mustard

## Directions

Place the boneless, skinless turkey breasts in a large-sized slow cooker. In a separate bowl, combine the remaining ingredients. Pour over turkey. Cover and cook on high for 4 hours. Let stand briefly before slicing. Serves 6 to 8.

# SLOW COOKER CHICKEN CACCIATORE

*This chicken dish is easy to assemble and set on low heat while you go out for several hours. You'll have a tender, moist chicken waiting for dinner when you come home. I like to make this on Sunday morning before we go for our nature walk in the park. When we get back, I'll refrigerate it and make the pasta later. We'll reheat our portions and serve it over freshly cooked vermicelli at dinner time.*

## Ingredients

5 to 6 boneless, skinless chicken thighs
2 cups sliced zucchini
1 green bell pepper, sliced
1 large onion, sliced
16 oz. sliced mushrooms
10 garlic cloves, peeled and halved
$1/4$ cup water
24 oz. jar spaghetti sauce
$1/2$ tsp. dried oregano
16 oz. Spaghetti, Vermicelli, or Angel Hair pasta
Olive oil
Garlic powder
Salt

## Directions

Place chicken in large slow cooker. Put vegetables on top. Add water, spaghetti sauce, and oregano. Cover and cook on low for 4 to 5 hours until chicken is tender. Meanwhile, cook the pasta according to package directions. Drain and add a tablespoon or so of olive oil to moisten and a sprinkle of garlic powder. Add salt to taste. Serve chicken dish over spaghetti. Makes 4 to 6 servings.

# SLOW COOKER CORNISH HENS

*This gives you a delightful variation on chicken when you'd like a poultry dish but want something different. I'll make this recipe as a special meal for Dalton when Brianna is away staying overnight with a friend. You should see the expression of joy that comes over his face when I set a plate with a whole hen at his table setting. Serve with your favorite side dishes. Add some candlelight for a romantic meal.*

## Ingredients

1 onion, chopped
6 oz. chopped celery
2 Cornish game hens, thawed in refrigerator
$1/_2$ tsp. garlic powder
$1/_2$ tsp. paprika
1 tsp. oregano
1 tsp. thyme
6 oz. baby carrots
24 oz. baby potatoes, halved
2 Tbsp. chopped fresh dill
$1/_4$ cup dry white wine

## Directions

Spray slow cooker insert with cooking spray. Add chopped onions and celery. Put hens on top of vegetables. Mix herbs in separate bowl and sprinkle on chicken. Add baby carrots, potatoes and dill. Pour white wine on top. Cover and cook on low for 8 hours. Serves 2.

# TURKEY BURGERS

*Dalton created this recipe, which is one of his favorites when he isn't grilling steaks or salmon outside. Serve with buns or without bread as per your choice. As a variation, try Worcestershire sauce instead of the soy sauce.*

## Ingredients

$1^1/_4$ lb. ground turkey
$^1/_2$ cup dry bread crumbs
4 green onions, minced
2 Tbsp. chopped fresh basil
2 Tbsp. fresh lime juice
1 Tbsp. soy sauce
2 tsp. garlic, minced

## Directions

Mix ingredients in large bowl. Shape mixture into balls. Flatten to make into burgers. Refrigerate until ready to grill. Brush or spray burgers with oil on both sides. Grill over direct medium heat for about 5 to 7 minutes, turning once, until cooked through. Serves 4.

# TURKEY MEATLOAF

*This savory meatloaf tastes just as good when reheated the next day. Meatloaf is comfort food at its best and is one of Dalton's favorite meals. Serve with mashed potatoes and a salad or sides of your choice.*

## Ingredients

2 Tbsp. olive oil
8 oz. container mixed chopped celery, onion, green pepper (trinity mix)
1 tsp. minced garlic
1 pound lean ground beef
1 pound ground turkey
1 Tbsp. tomato paste
$1/4$ cup dry bread crumbs
$1/2$ cup buttermilk
1 egg white
2 Tbsp. chopped fresh parsley
Barbecue sauce

## Directions

Preheat oven to 350 degrees. In a frying pan, sauté onion, celery and green pepper in oil until wilted. Add garlic and stir until fragrant. Turn off heat and set aside. Combine the rest of the ingredients in a large bowl. Add onion mixture and stir to blend. Fold into loaf pan and top with barbecue sauce. Bake for one hour. Slice and serve hot. Makes 4 to 6 servings.

# TURKEY TETRAZZINI

*This classic dish is the perfect use for turkey dinner leftovers. Or don't wait until you make a whole turkey and buy the prepared variety. It's good for feeding busy families because you'll get a few meals from this tasty recipe.*

## Ingredients

16 oz. spaghetti or vermicelli
2 cups cooked roast turkey or 8 oz. package Perdue carved turkey breast
2 Tbsp. olive oil
1 chopped onion
1 chopped green pepper
12 oz. fresh sliced mushrooms
10.5 oz. can cream of mushroom soup
12 oz. bag frozen mixed vegetables
4 oz. jar diced pimento, drained
1 cup shredded cheddar cheese
$1/_4$ cup dry white wine
1 Tbsp. Worcestershire sauce
$1/_2$ cup grated Parmesan cheese
Paprika

## Directions

Preheat oven to 375 degrees. Cook pasta according to package directions, drain, and set aside.

In a large skillet, heat oil. Sauté onion, green pepper, and mushrooms until wilted. Meanwhile, cut turkey into bite-size pieces and put into a large bowl along with cooked spaghetti.

145

Mix in onion, green pepper, and mushrooms, plus mushroom soup, mixed vegetables, pimento, cheddar cheese, white wine, and Worcestershire sauce. Mix well to blend.

Pour mixture into greased 10x14x2 inch baking dish. Sprinkle Parmesan cheese and paprika on top. Bake for 25 minutes, or until heated through. Serves 6 to 8.

# DEAD ROOTS

## Bad Hair Day Mystery #7

Dead Roots *does not contain recipes, but the story takes place over Thanksgiving weekend, so naturally there's a turkey dinner involved. Unfortunately, it turns out to be a less than festive event.*

### The Story

Hairstylist Marla Shore is hoping for a romantic interlude with her fiancé over Thanksgiving weekend at Sugar Crest Plantation Resort. She's eager to introduce him to her extended family during their stay at the haunted hotel. Their festive turkey dinner turns into a serious bad hair day when she finds her aunt suffocated in bed. It will take all of Marla's skills to untangle the clues and root out the killer, even if it means exposing her family's unsavory past.

### Excerpt from Dead Roots

Marla halted, shifting her feet while she mustered her courage. She studied a spot on the wall when she spoke. "I have some bad news. Aunt Polly... she passed away in her sleep."

Anita clutched a hand to her heart. "What?"

Moishe and William rose in unison. "You're saying our sister is gone?" Uncle William said, his voice hoarse.

Marla nodded, swallowing past a lump in her throat.

"I don't believe it," Anita cried. "We just spoke to her. She might have had memory lapses, but Polly didn't say anything about ill health other than normal complaints."

"Maybe she felt this coming on, and that's why she planned the reunion," Marla suggested.

"You could be right," Cousin Cynthia remarked. "She seemed adamant about coming to Sugar Crest."

Marla moved to her spot at the table. "Perhaps she wanted to die here in order to guard the family treasure with the other spirits. Which one of you hired the nurse's aide last night?"

Polly's siblings exchanged puzzled glances. "What are you talking about?" Anita asked.

"I was with Polly in her room when a health care worker arrived. She said someone had sent her as a gift for the evening." When no one admitted their generosity, Marla gave them all a scrutinizing glare. "If none of you paid for this woman, who did?"

"Call the service that sent her, and they'll tell you," offered Rochelle in a small voice. She sat at the far end flanked by their other young cousins.

"Do you suspect this aide had something to do with Polly's death?" Anita snapped.

"Who knows?" Marla sank into her chair, grabbed her wineglass, and drained the contents.

A waitress in a black dress and white apron approached. "Ma'am, would you like your dinner now? I've been holding it for you."

"Yes, thank you." It would be a while before their next meal, especially if their activities were cancelled in the wake of her aunt's death.

Her relatives plied her with questions to which she responded in monosyllables in between bites of turkey dinner. She wasn't terribly hungry but forced herself to eat. Another glass of wine left her light-headed but calmer.

Dr. Angus was probably right in assuming Polly had died of natural causes. If her aunt had to take morphine, she must have been hiding a serious problem. Perhaps she'd merely hastened her own death by taking too much of the narcotic. But then, who'd hired the aide and why were Polly's undergarments strewn across the floor?

Marla remembered her own evening purse had been displaced in the room she shared with Dalton. She *had* unpacked it and put it in a drawer. Somehow the beaded bag had made its way back into her suitcase. Person or poltergeist? Were there truly ghosts here, or were humans at fault, perpetuating the legends for their own purposes?

While her relatives discussed the latest family fiasco, she wondered if one of them lied about hiring the aide. It should be easy enough to discover who'd paid the bill if the woman had come from a service. Maybe she'd left a receipt in Polly's room.

*I'll have to get in there later, after things quiet down.* Among other items, Marla needed to obtain Polly's checkbook. Since her name was on the account, she'd have to pay any final bills. More importantly, she wanted to locate the letters her aunt had mentioned. Perhaps they gave a clue to Polly's illness, but that made sense only if they were recent.

No doubt about it, she needed access to Polly's personal belongings.

**ORDER NOW** at
https://nancyjcohen.com/dead-roots/

# ENTREES — FISH

# BAKED SALMON FILLETS

*Aunt Selma served this dish to us at her house, and it was so good that I had to ask for the recipe. To my surprise, it was amazingly easy to prepare. Another option is to use ranch dressing mixed with spicy brown mustard as the sauce. For added flavor, dip coated side of fish into finely chopped pecans or macadamia nuts.*

## Ingredients

1 1/2 pounds fresh salmon fillets
4 Tbsp. mayonnaise
4 Tbsp. chili sauce
Garlic powder
1 lemon, sliced

## Directions

Preheat oven to 400 degrees. Place salmon, skin side down, on greased 9x13x2 inch baking dish. In a small bowl, mix equal parts mayonnaise and chili sauce. Sprinkle in a shake of garlic powder. Spread sauce over fillets. Bake for 10 to 12 minutes or until cooked through, depending on how you like it done. Serve with fresh lemon slices. Serves 4.

# BAKED TILAPIA

*This healthy meal is quick to prepare. I learned all about tilapia breeding in* Body Wave, *where I went to interview a potential suspect in Tarpon Springs, Florida. Tilapia became one of my favorite fish choices to serve. I liked that it's raised on farms and doesn't feed on other fish.*

## Ingredients

4 tilapia fillets
14.5 oz. can diced low sodium tomatoes with basil, oregano, and garlic
4 oz. chopped onions
4 oz. chopped bell peppers
4 oz. sliced mushrooms

## Directions

Preheat oven to 350 degrees. Place tilapia fillets in a greased 9x13x2 inch baking dish. Spoon tomatoes over fish. Sprinkle on chopped onions, peppers and mushrooms. Cover and bake for 20 minutes or until fish is cooked through. Serves 4.

# DILLED SALMON PIE

*My mother served this recipe at a luncheon. I liked it so much that I made it at home. It's great as a brunch dish and is a savory way to use canned salmon. You can eat it for breakfast or lunch with sliced avocado or tomatoes. It also serves well as a light dinner with a salad. For a healthier choice, use reduced fat milk, and substitute fresh chopped dill for the dried variety. This pie may be frozen and reheated later in the oven or by the slice in the microwave.*

## Ingredients

(1) 9 inch deep dish pie crust, defrosted if frozen
2 Tbsp. butter
2 medium onions, chopped
1 Tbsp. chopped fresh parsley
$1/4$ tsp. dried dill
3 Tbsp. all purpose flour
$1/4$ tsp. salt
1 cup milk
$1/2$ cup shredded Swiss cheese
15.5 oz. can salmon, drained and flaked
$1/4$ cup dry bread crumbs

## Directions

Preheat oven to 400 degrees. Bake the unpricked pie crust for 5 minutes; remove and cool. Turn oven temperature down to 350 degrees.

In a medium saucepan, cook onions in 2 Tbsp. butter until translucent. Stir in parsley and dill. Blend in flour and salt.

Add milk all at once. Cook and stir until mixture is thickened and bubbly. Stir in cheese until melted. Gently fold in salmon.

Pour mixture into pie crust. Sprinkle bread crumbs on top of pie. Bake at 350 degrees for 30 minutes or until set. Let stand 5 minutes before serving. Serves 6.

# GARLIC SHRIMP SKEWERS

*This one is Dalton's specialty. He serves it with a prepared rice dish and a salad. It takes a bit of preparation time to put the skewers together, so it's good for a weekend dine-in meal.*

## Ingredients

1 to 2 lbs. jumbo shrimp, peeled and deveined, tails intact
16 large cloves garlic
$1/3$ cup olive oil
$1/4$ cup tomato sauce
2 Tbsp. red wine vinegar
2 Tbsp. chopped fresh basil
1 Tbsp. minced garlic

## Directions

Blanch whole garlic cloves in boiling water for 3 minutes. Remove garlic from pot and dunk in ice water. Peel and set aside. Meanwhile, in a large bowl, blend the olive oil, tomato sauce, red wine vinegar, chopped basil, and minced garlic. Add the peeled shrimp and toss to coat. Cover and refrigerate for 30 minutes.

Soak the skewers in water for 10 minutes. Heat the grill. Remove the shrimp from the bowl and thread them onto presoaked wood skewers. Curl shrimp so ends are nearly touching. Pierce the shrimp twice, just above tail and out the opposite side. Alternate on skewer with large garlic cloves. Option: Add grape tomatoes, mushrooms, zucchini slices, or onion chunks at this stage.

Place skewers on oiled grill rack 4-6 inches above the fire, turn frequently, and brush with remaining marinade. Grill for 6 to 10 minutes or until cooked through. Note: Shrimp skewers can be finished off or baked in the oven as an alternative. Serves 4 to 6.

# MACARONI SHRIMP SALAD

*Serve this recipe as a light summer meal or make a large bowl for a lunch buffet. It's a refreshing variation for shrimp lovers if you want to fix a one-dish salad.*

## Ingredients

16 oz. package elbow macaroni
1½ lb. cooked salad-size shrimp, peeled and deveined
16 oz. frozen peas
1 medium onion, chopped
Juice from 1/2 lemon
4 oz. jar diced pimento, drained

## Dressing

2 cups mayonnaise
2 Tbsp. sugar
½ cup ketchup
2 Tbsp. white wine vinegar
1½ tsp. paprika
1 to 2 tsp. garlic powder
Dash of Tabasco sauce

## Directions

Defrost shrimp if frozen. Cook macaroni according to package directions. Drain and set aside.

In a large bowl, combine cooked macaroni with shrimp, peas, onion, lemon juice, and pimento. In a separate bowl, whisk together dressing ingredients. Pour enough over shrimp salad to moisten and save the rest as extra dressing.

Cover and refrigerate before serving. This dish works well served on a platter with scoops of shrimp salad on top of lettuce and surrounded by your favorite cut veggies. Serves 6 to 8.

# SALMON CROQUETTES

*My mother made these mouth-watering salmon patties that she served with spaghetti and tomato sauce. I've gotten Dalton and Brianna to like them, too. I make sure to keep a couple of large cans of salmon in the pantry for when I get the desire to make this meal. If you don't have spaghetti handy, serve with your favorite side dish. It'll go just as well with rice or potatoes.*

## Ingredients

(2) 15 oz. cans pink or red salmon, drained
$1/_2$ tsp. garlic powder
$1/_4$ cup dry bread crumbs
$3/_4$ cup egg substitute
Olive oil

## Directions

Add salmon to large bowl. Remove bones if present. Flake salmon with fork. Add garlic powder, bread crumbs, and egg substitute. Mix thoroughly. Take a heaping tablespoonful in your hand and form mixture into patties. Place on a plate. Refrigerate prior to frying. Fry in olive oil in large skillet until crispy browned on both sides. Serves 4.

# SALMON POTATO BAKE

*Here's another good one for brunch. It's quick and easy to make and can be reheated for leftovers. Look for the potato pancake mix in the kosher section of your supermarket.*

## Ingredients

6 oz. box potato pancake mix
2 eggs
2 cups water
$1/4$ cup butter, melted
15 oz. can salmon, drained and flaked
$1/4$ cup grated Cheddar cheese

## Directions

Preheat oven to 350 degrees. In a large bowl, whisk eggs and water into the potato pancake mix. Let stand until thickened. Add melted butter and salmon. Stir to blend. Pour into a greased 9-inch square baking dish. Sprinkle cheese on top. Bake for 30 minutes or until edges are browned. Serves 4 to 6.

# SHRIMP BROWN RICE

*Here's a one-dish meal sure to satisfy with shrimp, rice and vegetables. It'll warm you up on a cold day or you can serve it as a light meal in warm weather.*

## Ingredients

1 to 2 lbs. cooked large shrimp, peeled and deveined
1 Tbsp. olive oil
1 medium onion, chopped
1 medium red bell pepper, chopped
16 oz. sliced mushrooms
2 cups uncooked brown rice
1 tsp. minced garlic
1 tsp. saffron powder
48 oz. low sodium chicken broth
12 oz. frozen broccoli florets, defrosted
8 oz. frozen peas

## Directions

Thaw shrimp if frozen. In a Dutch oven, sauté onion, red bell pepper, and mushrooms in oil until tender. Stir in the rice, garlic and saffron. Cook 1 to 2 minutes, then add broth. Bring to a boil, reduce heat, and simmer until liquid is absorbed, about 45 minutes. Add broccoli, peas, and shrimp, and cook until heated through. Serves 6 to 8.

# SHRIMP SALAD

*Try this different take on shrimp salad and serve to your guests at a luncheon. Add healthy accompaniments such as sliced red bell pepper strips, olives, or avocado slices.*

## Ingredients

2 cups cooked salad-size shrimp, peeled and deveined
2 hardboiled eggs, chopped
4 Tbsp. minced onion
$1/_2$ cup chopped celery
1 cup mayonnaise
2 Tbsp. Dijon mustard
1 tsp. dried tarragon
$1/_4$ tsp. dried dill
Dash of curry powder

## Directions

Thaw shrimp if frozen. Combine all ingredients in a bowl and mix together. Refrigerate for at least 4 hours to blend flavors. Serve on rolls for sandwiches; stuff in a large, ripe tomato; or serve on a bed of lettuce with your choice of garnish. Serves 4.

# THAI SHRIMP

*Are you a fan of Thai food? Even if you're not, you have to try this recipe. It's easy to make and delicious over a mound of cooked rice.*

## Ingredients

$1/_2$ lb. cooked large shrimp, peeled and deveined
4 Tbsp. lime juice, divided
2 shallots, chopped
2 tsp. minced fresh ginger
2 cloves garlic, chopped
2 Tbsp. olive oil
1 pint cherry or grape tomatoes, halved
16 oz. sliced mushrooms
$1/_2$ cup low sodium chicken broth
$1/_2$ cup coconut milk
2 tsp. curry powder
Cooked rice

## Directions

Thaw shrimp if frozen. Sprinkle shrimp with 2 Tbsp. lime juice. In a large skillet, sauté the shallots, ginger, and garlic in olive oil until wilted. Add tomatoes, mushrooms, broth, coconut milk, curry powder, and remaining lime juice and bring to a boil. Reduce heat and add shrimp. Add extra broth if more sauce is desired. Toss to coat shrimp and simmer uncovered until mushrooms are tender and shrimp is heated through. Serve over cooked rice. Makes 4 to 6 servings.

# TILAPIA DIJON

*This has become a favorite of mine since having it over my friend Tally's house. When you're a working woman, you don't have a lot of time to cook on weekdays. This recipe is quick and easy to make, and it even tastes good reheated the next day. Serve with your choice of sides.*

## Ingredients

4 tilapia fillets
2 Tbsp. light mayonnaise
2 Tbsp. grated Parmesan cheese
1 Tbsp. lemon juice
2 tsp. Dijon mustard
1 tsp. prepared fresh grated white horseradish
$1/4$ cup dry bread crumbs
2 Tbsp. butter, melted

## Directions

Preheat oven to 400 degrees. In a small bowl, combine the mayonnaise, 1 Tbsp. Parmesan cheese, lemon juice, mustard and horseradish. Put fillets in greased 9-inch square baking dish. Spread mixture over fish. Meanwhile, in another bowl, mix the bread crumbs, melted butter, and remaining 1 Tbsp. Parmesan cheese. Sprinkle over fish. Bake for 20 minutes or until fish is cooked through. Serves 4.

# TUNA CHINESE CASSEROLE

*My mother served this meal to my brother and me when we were growing up. Keep these ingredients in stock for when you're in the mood for Chinese food but don't feel like going out. It's easy to make and satisfies your stomach.*

## Ingredients

(2) 5 oz. cans chunk light tuna, drained and flaked
14 oz. can chop suey vegetables, drained
10.5 oz. can cream of mushroom soup
$1/_2$ cup fat free milk
3 hard-boiled eggs, chopped
5 oz. can chow mein noodles
Grated Parmesan cheese
Cooked rice

## Directions

Preheat oven to 375 degrees. Mix first five ingredients in large bowl. Pour into greased 2-quart casserole dish. Sprinkle noodles and Parmesan cheese on top. Bake for 30 minutes or until bubbling. Option: Add a can of peas. Serve over cooked rice. Makes 4 servings.

# TUNA PEA CASSEROLE

*This makes an attractive company dish for lunch when baked and served in shell-shaped ovenware. Recipe may be multiplied. If you keep the ingredients in stock, it's a quick throw-together meal accompanied by a pre-made salad.*

## Ingredients

(2) 12 oz. cans tuna, drained and flaked
8.5 oz. can peas, drained
10.5 oz. can cream of mushroom soup
2 Tbsp. dry bread crumbs
2 Tbsp. grated Parmesan cheese

## Directions

Mix first three ingredients in a microwave-safe bowl. Sprinkle bread crumbs and Parmesan cheese on top. Microwave for 3 to 5 minutes on high or until heated through. Serves 2 to 4.

# TUNA RICE SUPREME

*One-dish meals are always appealing, especially when they're as easy to prepare as this tasty entrée. Serve plated or in a bowl and watch your family members reach for a second portion.*

## Ingredients

2 cups uncooked long grain rice
12 oz. can tuna
6 oz. shredded sharp cheddar cheese
16 oz. frozen mixed vegetables
8 oz. chopped onions
(2) 10.5 oz. cans cream of mushroom soup
1 small can mushroom pieces
4 oz. jar diced pimento, drained
Grated Parmesan cheese

## Directions

Preheat oven to 350 degrees. Prepare rice according to package directions. Set aside. Flake tuna in large bowl. Add remaining ingredients plus rice. Pour mixture into greased 9x13x2 inch baking dish. Sprinkle Parmesan cheese on top. Bake until warm and bubbly, about 30 minutes. Serves 4.

# TUNA SPAGHETTI PIE

*If you want to make a spaghetti pie without the usual beef combo, try this meal that uses tuna instead. Serve this attractive dish for brunch or lunch, or as a light dinner with a salad.*

## Ingredients

Crust
8 oz. cooked spaghetti
1/4 cup grated Parmesan cheese
1 egg, lightly beaten
1 Tbsp. butter, softened
1 tsp. chopped garlic

Filling
1 Tbsp. chopped onion
1 Tbsp. butter, melted
1 Tbsp. all-purpose flour
1/4 tsp. garlic powder
1/4 cup reduced fat milk
1/4 cup light sour cream
1 egg, beaten
6 oz. can tuna, drained and flaked
1/4 cup grated Parmesan cheese
1 tomato, thinly sliced

## Directions

Preheat oven to 350 degrees. In a large bowl, mix together the first five ingredients. Press onto the bottom and sides of a greased 9-inch pie dish. Set aside.

In a skillet, sauté the onion in butter until wilted. Remove from heat. Stir in the flour and garlic powder. In a separate bowl, beat the milk, sour cream, and egg with a whisk until blended. Stir into the onion mixture. Fold in the tuna.

Spoon filling into crust. Sprinkle half the remaining Parmesan cheese over the pie. Arrange tomato slices on top. Sprinkle on the rest of the Parmesan cheese. Bake for 40 minutes or until crust is golden brown. Serves 6.

# TUNA SPAGHETTI SALAD

*My mother taught me this recipe as it's usually her favorite for a pot-luck luncheon. She'll double the ingredients to make it stretch and will refrigerate it until needed. As the flavors blend, this dish tastes even better.*

## Ingredients

8 oz. uncooked spaghetti
(2) 12 oz. cans solid white tuna in water, drained and flaked
14.5 oz. can petite diced tomatoes, drained
4 oz. jar diced pimento, drained
1 cup celery, chopped
1 cup pitted black olives, chopped
1 cup sweet onion, chopped
$3/4$ cup mayonnaise or more as needed
4 tsp. lemon juice
Bunch of fresh parsley

## Directions

Cook spaghetti according to package directions. Drain and place in bowl. Cut into shorter pieces. In a separate large bowl, add the rest of ingredients except for parsley and toss lightly. Mix in spaghetti. Cover and refrigerate until ready to serve. Spoon into a serving bowl and garnish with parsley sprigs. Serve cold. Makes 4 to 6 servings.

# BODY WAVE

## Bad Hair Day Mystery #4

Body Wave *doesn't contain recipes, but it features tilapia and explains how this fish is farmed. In this excerpt, Marla and Dalton are speaking to Jeremiah Dooley, a shady televangelist who runs a tilapia farm in Tarpon Springs, Florida.*

**The Story**

Hairstylist Marla Shore goes undercover in a hair-brained scheme to catch a killer in her latest South Florida adventure. In a story braided with unexpected twists and curls, she takes on a role as nurse's aide for wealthy Miriam Pearl. While Marla snoops into the elderly matriarch's affairs, her boyfriend, Detective Dalton Vail, is afraid that the only affair she'll snag is with her ex-spouse, Stan. Juggling work at her salon, crime solving, and two amorously inclined males, Marla fights a race against time to save Stan before the dashing detective nails him for murder.

**Excerpt from Body Wave**

"Tilapia have been raised as far back as ancient Egypt. Legend tells us that tilapia was the fish our Lord multiplied to feed the masses. Since it comes from the Nile River, this is probably true. Tilapia is the most popular fish in freshwater aquaculture because it's so hardy and easy to breed."

"Really? What does that mean in terms of production values?" Marla asked, attempting to gauge his organization's financial status.

"Just to give you an idea, annual yield in the United States approximates twenty million pounds," Jeremiah said, puncturing his remarks with gestures. "In Florida, fish farms produce over one million pounds per year. Let me add that tilapia is a tropical fish."

Marla cast a glance at Dalton. While she'd kept Jeremiah occupied, he had sidled over to peer at a stack of papers on the minister's desk. She could tell he was more interested in the office accoutrements than the fish tanks. *Okay, I can play this game, she told him silently.*

"What happens with temperature variations?" she queried, plastering a look of rapt fascination on her face.

"Warm water increases their growth rate. Cold weather can kill them if the water temperature drops below fifty degrees."

"What are these different types?"

The reverend pointed to each tank in turn, speaking like a professor to a student. "This is blue tilapia, which is naturalized in Florida and inhabits the Everglades. That's white tilapia, and the other one is a hybrid of Nile tilapia. You can tell by its stripes. The hybrid is also more aggressive."

"I'm curious," Dalton said from the opposite side of the room. "If you direct your activities from this location, where do you film your television shows?"

Jeremiah puffed out his chest. "I live in Margate, and I do the shows from a studio in Miami. Regarding the missions, we have a manager who oversees our business operations, and an aquaculture specialist who supervises the farms. So I only come up here on special occasions, to meet folks like you or to make sure everything is running smoothly." His eyes narrowed, as though he'd just noticed Dalton wasn't listening to his lecture. "You said you're from Palm Haven, but I didn't catch the name of your company."

Dalton had a ready answer. "I'm in security, and Marla owns a chain of hair salons. Why don't you give the good reverend one of your business cards, sweetcakes?"

She returned his dazzling smile with a conspiratorial wink. Handing Jeremiah a card, she said, "This is for my anchor store. Come in sometime, and I'll give you a complementary cut."

The minister's hair didn't have a single strand out of place. He must use a generous share of his pocket money on hair spray. Her glance took in his manicured fingernails. No wonder he didn't work on the farm; it might soil his hands. She hoped to kick up some dirt herself while they were here.

"My friend mentioned your show," Marla ventured. "Her name was Kimberly Kaufman. Maybe you read about her in the newspapers since you live near Fort Lauderdale. She was murdered a couple of weeks ago."

"How horrible," Jeremiah said, steepling his hands in a prayer position.

"Kim said she knew you personally."

Jeremiah glanced from Marla to Dalton, who was engaged in casually picking off a fleck of lint from his shirt. "We'd met a couple of times. Like yourself, Mrs. Kaufman was interested in donating to the cause. I always try to meet our benefactors in person."

"Did you attend her funeral?"

"No, I wasn't on intimate terms with the family. When I didn't hear from Mrs. Kaufman again, I just assumed she'd lost interest. I'm so sorry to hear she met such a dreadful end."

*If you weren't intimate, why did she call you Uncle Jerry?* "How did you meet each other? Did Kim contact you?"

"You seem mighty interested in my relations with your friend, Miz Shore."

Marla tilted her head. "If it weren't for Kimberly, Dalton and I wouldn't have known about your work. We've always been concerned about world hunger, so we were thrilled to learn about your efforts. Breeding fish in ponds is an excellent means of providing food for thousands."

She'd hit upon the right subject to divert him. "You're absolutely right. Praise the Lord for his gift." Jeremiah raised

175

his arms. "He giveth us the means to produce a bounty of consumables. Who needs material wealth when we have food stocks? You can't eat money."

*No, but you can buy a Porsche with it.* From the corner of her eye, she watched Dalton shift a few papers on the file cabinet. "Do many people know about tilapia?" she asked to grab Jeremiah's attention. "I've seen it on the menu at restaurants."

He gave her a benevolent smile. "Look for it in the fish counters of your local grocery store, too. Tilapia is rapidly gaining consumer recognition. Besides being white, firm, and moist, it's mild in flavor, so it accepts sauces well. You can use it in recipes that specify other kinds of fish. Let's go outside, and I'll show you the rest."

Nodding agreeably, Marla hoped her companion noticed how well they worked as a team. A moment's guilt flushed through her at their deception. Dalton had arranged this meeting under false pretenses. It was bad enough that Marla had deceived the Pearl family in her role as nurse's aide. She dreaded the day Miriam would discover her ruse, especially since she'd become fond of the woman. Maybe the reverend would give her a blessing and absolve her from sin.

*Yeah, right. Believe that, and you can make hair sprout on a bald head with a prayer.*

They emerged into the sunshine on a raised walkway. Marla was aware of Dalton's presence directly behind her. When he placed a possessive hand on her shoulder, she folded into him, leaning against the solid length of his body. His arm curved around, encompassing her waist. A slight smile lifted the reverend's lips as he regarded the intimate gesture.

"We grow tilapia in outdoor tanks and ponds since our weather is fairly predictable," Jeremiah continued, squinting in the bright light. "Other farms may use greenhouses to control the climate, but we don't worry about that here. I mentioned that tilapia is a hardy fish. Since they have strong immune systems, they're more easily grown than other fish species that are prone to disease, plus they don't get as stressed by environmental changes. These factors make tilapia a highly marketable, protein-rich food source as well as a cash-generating crop, so it's perfect for our third-world missions."

"Don't you have sites in Costa Rica?" Marla adjusted her purse strap as they walked on.

He nodded. "Our farms there use pure rainwater from the cloud forests. It flows by gravity through the farms at such a rate that the ponds exchange their water every twenty minutes."

"Is the fish sold there or exported?"

"We harvest the fish six days a week. Some of it is distributed locally and the rest is flown to Miami each evening. From there, we deliver the fish to customers by truck or air."

"Kimberly's family owns coffee plantations in Costa Rica," Dalton commented in a dry tone.

"Really? What a coincidence." Jeremiah gripped the black metal railing that lined the walkway.

"Are you acquainted with Morris Pearl?" Dalton asked. "He's the family member who runs their business."

"Sorry, never heard of him."

"Where did you say you lived in Fort Lauderdale?"

"Margate." The reverend frowned at Dalton. "I don't understand why you're asking these questions. I thought you wanted a tour of our facilities before making a contribution. Perhaps you're ready to conclude our business."

Marla felt Dalton stiffen and stepped away from him. "How long does it take for the tilapia to grow?" she said in a ditzy tone, hoping to ease the sudden tension that had sprung up between the two men.

Jeremiah seemed happy to resume his didactic role. Plowing a hand through his styled hair, he said, "It takes six to twelve months for them to reach full size. We harvest them when they reach a pound and a half."

"How often do they reproduce?"

"Too often." Jeremiah laughed, and the tenseness dissipated like a flock of egrets taking flight. "Tilapia are mouth breeders. Normally, the male digs a nest in the sand. By flashing his tail, he attracts the female, who lays eggs. He fertilizes them, then she picks them up in her mouth and holds them until they hatch, which takes a couple of weeks. She can carry up to one thousand babies, called fry, in her mouth. An average female hatches over three hundred fingerlings every month year-round. Considering this rate of reproduction, you see how overpopulation becomes a problem."

"How much do they sell for?" Dalton asked.

"Tilapia can bring up to two dollars per pound. We sell our crop wholesale to seafood brokers, fish markets, restaurants. It's a more valuable commodity than something like catfish."

"Why isn't the water clear?" Marla pointed to one of the concrete tanks. The water was too deep and murky for her to see any fish swimming in it.

"That greenish tint is due to algae. It forms from sunlight penetrating to the bottom. The young fish feed on algae. Tiny combs in their gills allow them to remove it from the water. They have efficient digestive systems and convert a greater proportion of their food into growth than many other fish species."

"They don't eat anything else?"

"We provide fish food that comes in different formulations to match their growth stage. We're careful to buy a product containing marine and vegetable protein, with no terrestrial animal parts. Come this way." He led them up a short flight of stairs and along a maze of elevated walkways, pipes and hoses, netting and buckets. They detoured around workers engaged in various tasks. All of them deferentially made way for the minister and his guests.

"Besides the algae, tannin and fish poop alter the clarity of the water." Jeremiah chuckled at Marla's grimace. "When we're ready to harvest, we put the fish into a tank of clear water to flush the metabolites from their systems. This purges toxins so no odor remains. That process takes two or three days. Because they don't feed on other fish, which might contain pollutants, tilapia is one of the cleanest varieties."

"According to what you're saying, the tilapia are only as pure as their water supply," Dalton cut in, draping his arm around Marla's shoulder.

"Good point." The reverend speared him with a keen glance. "Our water passes through a filtration process beginning with a biofilter system. After passing through particle settling and nitrogen conversion tanks, the water sifts through a micron particle filter to remove fine fragments. Then it's mixed with oxygen and pumped into the fish tanks."

Marla sought a way to bring up Kimberly again, but this didn't seem an appropriate time. Dalton seemed content to play along with their ruse for now. His sharp gaze surveyed their surroundings, absorbing details.

They headed down a dirt path, kicking up dust. "This is our raceway section for high-density production of tilapia, eels, and sturgeon," Jeremiah explained.

"I noticed eel tanks in the building earlier," Dalton said, scooping Marla's hand into his. She gave him a startled glance. Wasn't he overplaying his role? Not that she'd dare protest, since Jeremiah seemed taken in by their act. What she saw in Dalton's eyes wasn't pretense, however. A coil of desire snaked its way through her body as she squeezed his hand in response.

"Eels are very popular for sushi," Jeremiah answered, beaming at them. "They sell for five to nine dollars per pound wholesale. Since birds like to eat them, we have to protect our outdoor tanks with netting. You'll find up to ten thousand eels in one tank. They grow into small, medium, or large sizes."

"How did you become so knowledgeable about all this?" Dalton asked on their way back to the main building.

*Yes, Dalton. Now that Jeremiah is off guard, slam him with the real questions.* Marla avoided looking at him, afraid she'd smile and give away their game.

"I studied marine biology before receiving my calling. I think the good Lord meant it that way. He gave me the means to feed thousands and provide work for our less fortunate brethren."

"How did you arrive in Tarpon Springs? I thought mostly Greeks lived here."

"My father was Greek, not that it matters. People move here for different reasons."

"Your last name is Irish."

"It's my mother's name. She didn't change it on the birth certificate."

"Piotr didn't mind?"

Jeremiah stopped, his expression darkening. "How do you know his name? Have you been checking up on me?"

"Before I give money to anyone, I always investigate," Dalton replied.

The minister led them inside his office. "I hope you're satisfied by what you saw today. You can make your check out to Ministry of Hope."

*Gone is the smooth-talking representative of the Lord. Here is the true huckster in prime form.* Marla wondered how Dalton would get out of this one.

"I'll have to get back to you," Dalton said. "You're doing some wonderful work here, but I'm not sure you need the extra funding. Your operations must produce plenty of income."

"Any funds we generate are funneled right back into our missions." Jeremiah stood facing them. "We work among the poor in third-world countries. Our aim is to feed and house our farm workers in addition to the missionaries and their families. It's never enough when you're doing the Lord's work."

Dalton pulled out his wallet. But instead of offering the reverend a signed check, he showed him a photograph. "Recognize these people?"

The minister's face paled. "Where did you get this?"

"From Stan Kaufman, Kimberly's husband. He said you called on her one day, but she wasn't home. He recognized you in this photograph found in her room. Neighbors claimed they saw your car a couple of times in the neighborhood. They said Kim bragged about her rich Uncle Jerry. She was pregnant, Mr. Dooley. I suspect you were involved with Mrs. Kaufman in a manner your congregation would not condone. Were you the father of her child?"

Jeremiah's mouth gaped like a fish out of water. His skin turned the color of a white tilapia. "W-who are you?"

Dalton ignored his inquiry. "Where were you on the morning of February fifth?"

"Get out. Both of you, leave n-now," Jeremiah sputtered.

"You paid for Kim to go to design school, didn't you?" Marla said. "After she told you she was pregnant, you tried to buy her silence. It would be easy enough for her to pass the child off as Stan's. But Kim wanted to leave her husband. Did she threaten you? Is that why you killed her?"

The reverend clenched a pen in his hand. He stepped toward her, a menacing light in his mud brown eyes. "You'd better not spread these lies to anyone, or I'll scale you alive."

**ORDER NOW** at
https://nancyjcohen.com/body-wave/

# ENTREES — VEGETARIAN

# EGGPLANT PARMESAN

*If you're an eggplant fan, you must try this one. This recipe will have you wanting more in a heartbeat. It's a bit labor intensive but well worth the effort. Dalton and Brianna surprised me one weekend by following the recipe, and it came out perfectly. The kitchen wasn't so lucky. It took me at least a half hour to clean up afterward. Let's say the dishwasher came in handy. Serve this meal with a Caesar salad and garlic bread for the full Italian vibe.*

## Ingredients

1 large firm eggplant
Salt
$1/_2$ cup all-purpose flour
2 eggs, beaten or egg substitute equivalent
$1/_2$ cup dry bread crumbs
8 oz. package mozzarella cheese slices
24 oz. jar spaghetti sauce
$1/_2$ tsp. dried oregano
$1/_2$ cup grated Parmesan cheese

## Directions

Preheat oven to 350 degrees. Peel eggplant and cut cross-wise into one-half inch rounds. Salt eggplant slices on both sides and let sit for 20 minutes. Rinse off bitter juices and pat dry with paper towel. Sprinkle half of flour, eggs, and bread crumbs into three separate plates. Dip eggplant slices progressively in flour, eggs, and then bread crumbs. Add more of these ingredients as needed until all eggplant slices are coated.

Arrange eggplant rounds in greased baking pan and bake until fork goes through and slices are tender, about 15 minutes. Flip over halfway through cooking time. Remove from oven when done.

Spread thin layer of spaghetti sauce on bottom of greased 9x13x2 inch baking dish. Arrange half of eggplant slices over sauce, then cover with half of mozzarella cheese slices. Add another layer of sauce, eggplant, and mozzarella. Top with remaining sauce. Sprinkle with oregano and Parmesan cheese. Bake until heated through and bubbly, about 20 minutes. Serves 6 to 8.

# EGGPLANT ROLLATINI

*If you want to impress company with an Italian meal, make them this dish. It may seem a bit complicated but isn't really difficult to make. The key is to get the eggplant pliable enough to work with but not so soggy that it falls apart. Serve as above with Caesar salad and fresh baked garlic bread.*

## Ingredients

1 large firm eggplant
Salt
$1/2$ cup part-skim ricotta cheese
$1/2$ cup grated Parmesan cheese
1 large egg
1 tsp. minced garlic
2 cups tomato basil sauce
4 oz. shredded mozzarella cheese

## Directions

Peel eggplant and cut lengthwise into half-inch slices. Salt eggplant slices and let sit for 20 minutes. Rinse off bitter juices and pat dry with paper towel. In a microwave-safe dish, lay out eggplant. Microwave on high for 6 to 8 minutes until pliable. Transfer to plate and drain liquid from baking dish. Pat eggplant slices dry. In a separate bowl, combine ricotta and Parmesan cheeses, egg, and minced garlic. Mix together.

Starting at the wide end of each eggplant slice, spread a teaspoon of the cheese mixture. Roll up each piece and lay seam-side down in greased microwave-safe baking dish. Pour sauce over all.
Cover and microwave on high for 15 minutes or until eggplant

is tender. Sprinkle mozzarella cheese on top. Microwave until cheese melts, about 2 more minutes. Optional: Add a sprinkle of oregano and fresh chopped basil leaves before cooking. Serves 4 to 6.

# EGGPLANT TOMATO CASSEROLE

*My reading tastes lean toward* Modern Salon *and other related business trade journals, so I don't have time for cooking magazines. However, I saw this recipe inside a women's magazine at a doctor's office. Rather than tearing out the page, I took a picture on my cell phone. My family liked this healthy non-meat dish that I served with a side salad.*

## Ingredients

1 large firm eggplant
2 large tomatoes, sliced
1 large sweet onion, thinly sliced
0.75 oz. package fresh basil, trimmed
3 Tbsp. extra virgin olive oil
3 Tbsp. balsamic vinegar
8 oz. package mozzarella cheese slices
$1/2$ cup dry bread crumbs
$1/4$ cup grated Parmesan cheese

## Directions

Preheat oven to 400 degrees. Peel eggplant and cut lengthwise into half-inch slices. Salt eggplant slices and let sit for 20 minutes. Rinse off bitter juices and pat dry with paper towel. Grease a 9x13x2 inch baking dish. Layer the eggplant, tomatoes, and onions. Sprinkle basil leaves over eggplant mixture. Dribble with olive oil and balsamic vinegar.

Cover and bake at 400 degrees for 20 minutes. Remove cover. Put mozzarella cheese slices over mixture, then sprinkle with bread crumbs and Parmesan cheese. Bake uncovered for 15 minutes until cheese is melted and bubbly. Serves 6 to 8.

# EGGPLANT TORTELLINI

*You can substitute a container of pre-sliced zucchini for convenience if you wish. This dish goes well with a salad and another vegetable like fresh asparagus or broccoli.*

## Ingredients

1 large eggplant, peeled and cut into cubes
1 medium onion, sliced
1 large zucchini, peeled and sliced
1 cup water
24 oz. jar marinara sauce
(2) 10 oz. packages refrigerated cheese tortellini

## Directions

Lightly coat a Dutch oven with cooking spray. Add the eggplant, onion, and zucchini, and cook over medium-high heat for 5 to 10 minutes. Stir frequently. Add water, cover, and simmer until vegetables are tender, about 15 minutes more. Remove cover, add marinara sauce and stir. Mix in tortellini. Cover and cook on medium heat for another 8 minutes. Serves 6 to 8.

# MUSHROOM PIE

*This recipe is delicious as an appetizer or a brunch dish. Mushroom lovers will enjoy the rich flavor. My mother made it for me after she ate it at a Mah Jongg game with friends and asked her hostess for the recipe. You could also serve this mushroom pie as a side to a main entrée.*

## Ingredients

16 oz. sliced fresh mushrooms
8 oz. sliced fresh Portobello mushrooms
2 large shallots, peeled and diced
2 Tbsp. olive oil
1 cup grated Parmesan cheese
$\frac{1}{2}$ cup shredded Swiss cheese
(2) 9-inch deep dish pie crusts, defrosted if frozen
Egg Substitute

## Directions

Preheat oven to 350 degrees. Sauté mushrooms and shallots in olive oil in large skillet. Remove from heat. Mix in Parmesan and Swiss cheeses. Pour the mixture into one pie crust. Fold other pie crust over top. Brush with egg substitute. Bake for 30 to 45 minutes or until cooked through and browned. Slice and serve warm. Makes 4 to 6 servings.

# MUSHROOM POTATO SAVORY

*Serve this meal for brunch, or add a salad for a meat-free dinner. It gives you eggs, potatoes, and mushrooms all in one tasty dish. Be careful and don't make the mistake I did. When the oven timer went off after the first 25 minutes, I must have turned the oven off as well as the timer. I added the rest of the ingredients as directed and put the dish back in the oven to bake. After 45 minutes went by, the meal still wasn't set. The oven was warm but suspiciously not hot. I turned the temperature up to 400 degrees and let the mixture cook for a half hour more until done. So in case yours doesn't set after the time below, you can turn up the temperature and cook it for a short while more.*

## Ingredients

6 oz. box potato pancake mix
2 large eggs
$2^1/_4$ cups cold water
16 oz. sliced Portobello mushrooms, coarsely chopped
8 oz. container diced red onions
1 cup reduced fat milk
1 cup shredded sharp cheddar cheese
1 cup shredded Swiss cheese
5 large eggs

## Directions

Preheat oven to 350 degrees. In a medium bowl, beat 2 eggs with a fork. Add cold water. Stir in contents of potato pancake mix. Let stand to thicken.

Spread the potatoes along the bottom of a greased 9-inch square baking dish. Bake for 25 minutes or until lightly browned.

In a separate large bowl, combine all other ingredients. Pour on top of potatoes. Bake for 45 minutes or until bubbly. Serves 6 to 8.

# MUSHROOMS FLORENTINE

*I tried this dish as a vegetarian meal accompanied by a salad, but Dalton complained there wasn't any protein. He didn't believe me when I said the cheese counted that way. You could either serve this as an entrée alone or as a side dish for dinner, or as a starter course when you have company.*

## Ingredients

8 Portobello mushrooms
7 oz. jar pesto sauce
10 oz. package frozen chopped spinach, thawed and squeezed dry
1 cup ricotta cheese
1 cup chopped tomatoes
4 tsp. balsamic vinegar

## Directions

Preheat oven to 350 degrees. Line a 12x17x1 inch baking sheet or another suitable size pan with aluminum foil and spray with cooking spray. Remove stems from mushrooms and scrape out gills from underside. Rinse mushrooms to clean and pat dry with paper towels. Place mushrooms stem side up on greased baking sheet.

In a medium bowl, combine pesto sauce, spinach, and ricotta cheese. Spread mixture among mushroom caps. Top each one with a sprinkle of tomatoes and balsamic vinegar.

Bake, uncovered, for 20 minutes or until filling is melted and mixture is heated through. Serves 4 as a main meal or 8 as an appetizer.

# SPAGHETTI SQUASH WITH PEAS AND MUSHROOMS

*You can serve this as a vegetarian meal or as a side dish instead of pasta or potatoes. Cousin Cynthia created this recipe when she was on her weight-loss diet. She learned the hard way to pierce a squash before cooking so it doesn't explode.*

## Ingredients

1 spaghetti squash
3 Tbsp. olive oil
1 medium onion, chopped
1 tsp. minced garlic
8 oz. mushrooms, sliced
15 oz. package frozen petite green peas
$1/_2$ tsp. dried oregano
$1/_3$ cup freshly grated Parmesan cheese

## Directions

With a sharp knife, pierce the skin of the squash in at least 5 places. Place the squash on a microwave-safe dish and microwave on high for 10 minutes or until tender. Set aside until cool enough to handle. Then cut squash in half lengthwise and discard seeds. Using a fork, scrape the squash out in strands, like spaghetti.

Meanwhile, sauté the onion, garlic, and mushrooms in olive oil. Add frozen peas and stir until thawed. Add oregano, squash strands, and grated cheese to the vegetable mixture. Toss until everything is heated through and cheese is melted. Serves 4 to 6.

# SPINACH-STUFFED SHELLS

*If you want to serve an Italian meal that looks impressive but isn't hard to make, try this one. If you have any filling left over, use it to make stuffed mushrooms. Or bake it in a small casserole dish until heated through and serve with crackers as a dip.*

## Ingredients

1 box jumbo pasta shells
10 oz. frozen chopped spinach, thawed and squeezed dry
15 oz. ricotta cheese
$1/_2$ cup grated Parmesan cheese
1 egg
24 oz. jar marinara sauce
0.75 oz. package fresh basil, trimmed
1 cup shredded mozzarella cheese

## Directions

Preheat oven to 350 degrees. Grease a 9x13x2 inch baking dish. Cook the pasta shells according to package directions. Drain and set aside. Break up the spinach with a fork in a bowl. In another bowl, mix the ricotta and Parmesan cheese and the egg. Add spinach and blend well.

When shells are cool enough to handle, stuff each shell with one tsp. each of ricotta mixture. Spread enough tomato sauce on bottom of baking dish to lightly coat surface. Add the shells. Cover with remaining sauce, fresh basil, and mozzarella cheese. Bake at 350 degrees for 30 minutes or until edges are bubbly. Serves 6 to 8.

# TOMATO BROCCOLI QUICHE

*Quiches are too often relegated to ladies' luncheons as they're not considered manly enough for a guy's appetite. But Dalton likes this one that I'll serve for a weekend brunch. You can cut the calories further by omitting the pie shell and pouring the filling directly into a greased pie plate.*

## Ingredients

(1) 9-inch deep dish pie crust
1 Tbsp. olive oil
1 medium onion, chopped
1 tsp. minced garlic
10 oz. fresh or frozen chopped broccoli, thawed
$1^1/_2$ cups shredded Swiss cheese
1 Tbsp. flour
4 eggs, lightly beaten
$^3/_4$ cup heavy cream
$1^1/_4$ cups reduced fat milk
1 large tomato, thinly sliced

## Directions

Defrost and pre-bake the pie crust according to package directions. Set aside. Sauté the onion in olive oil in a medium skillet until wilted. Add garlic and broccoli and cook until broccoli is tender. Remove pan from heat. In a small bowl, combine the Swiss cheese and flour. In another medium bowl, mix the eggs, cream, and milk. Add the cheese mixture and then the broccoli. Stir to blend. Pour the mixture into the pie crust. Top with tomato slices.

Bake at 325 degrees for 60 minutes or until cooked through and browned. A toothpick inserted in center should come out clean. Serves 6.

# VEGETABLE GUMBO

*This hearty vegetarian dish can warm you on a winter night or help you watch your weight if you're counting calories. Add any fresh vegetables you have in stock if desired or substitute favorites for items below. Serve with a side salad.*

## Ingredients

3 Tbsp. olive oil
8 oz. container mixed chopped celery, onion, green pepper (trinity mix)
1 Tbsp. minced garlic
1 large bay leaf
$1/_4$ tsp. dried thyme
36 oz. vegetable broth
1 lb. sliced zucchini
28 oz. can crushed tomatoes
15 oz. can baby corn, drained
1 lb. peeled, cubed butternut squash
$1^1/_2$ cups Arborio rice
15.5 oz. can red kidney beans, drained and rinsed
2 Tbsp. chopped fresh parsley

## Directions

Heat oil in large soup pan over medium high heat. Add celery, onions, and green peppers along with garlic. Cook for 7 minutes. Add bay leaf and thyme and cook for 2 more minutes. Add vegetable broth, stir and bring to a boil. Add zucchini, tomatoes, baby corn, and squash. Reduce heat and simmer for 5 minutes. Stir in rice.

199

Simmer covered for another 20 minutes, stirring occasionally so rice doesn't stick to bottom. Mix in beans and parsley and cook for 5 minutes more, or until rice is done. Serves 6 to 8.

# VEGETABLE LASAGNE

*Tally served this once at a dinner party, and it was amazing. I asked for the recipe, even though it's a bit labor intensive. Vegetable lasagna is a healthy alternative to a classic dish.*

## Ingredients

12 no-cook lasagna noodles
12 oz. shredded Italian blend cheeses

Vegetables
2 medium zucchini, peeled and sliced in rounds
2 cups broccoli florets
2 large carrots, julienned
2 red bell peppers, julienned
2 tsp. chopped garlic
$3/4$ tsp. dried thyme
$1/4$ cup olive oil

Sauce
1 large onion, chopped
16 oz. Portobello mushrooms, sliced
2 tsp. chopped garlic
2 Tbsp. olive oil
(2) 28 oz. cans crushed tomatoes
3 tsp. Italian seasoning
2 Tbsp. chopped fresh basil

Filling
$1 1/4$ cups ricotta cheese
8 oz. package cream cheese, room temperature
1 egg
$3/4$ cup grated Parmesan cheese

Nancy J. Cohen

**Directions**

Preheat oven to 400 degrees. Put seven vegetable ingredients into a bowl and mix to blend. Spread over two greased baking sheets. Bake for 20 minutes or until tender. Set aside. Meanwhile, in a Dutch oven, sauté onions, mushrooms, and garlic in 2 Tbsp. olive oil until tender. Then stir in crushed tomatoes, Italian seasoning, and fresh basil leaves. Simmer for 15 minutes.

In a separate bowl, combine the filling ingredients. Grease a 9x13x2 inch baking pan. Spread 1 cup of sauce on the bottom of the baking dish. Layer with noodles, cheese filling, vegetables, and sauce. Sprinkle shredded Italian cheeses on top. Bake at 350 degrees for 40 minutes or until bubbly. Serves 6 to 8.

# VEGETABLE QUICHE

*For guests who wish to avoid dairy, this version is a cheese-free variation. It might require a little more work but is worth the effort.*

## Ingredients

(1) 9-inch deep dish pie crust, defrosted if frozen
1 Tbsp. olive oil
1 small onion, chopped
1 red bell pepper, diced
5 to 10 asparagus spears, trimmed & cut into 1-inch pieces
6 eggs
3 Tbsp. all-purpose flour
$1/2$ tsp. baking powder
$3/4$ cup unsweetened almond milk
$1/2$ tsp. salt
$1/2$ tsp. paprika
$1/2$ tsp. dried thyme
1 package fresh baby spinach

## Directions

Preheat oven to 350 degrees. Use a fork to prick a few holes in the pie crust and bake for 10 minutes. Remove and set aside. Meanwhile, heat olive oil in large sauté pan over medium-high heat. Add chopped onion, pepper and asparagus, and sauté for 5 minutes, or until onions are translucent and asparagus is fork-tender. Remove from heat.

In a separate large bowl, whisk together the eggs, flour, baking powder, almond milk, salt, paprika, and thyme. Stir in sautéed vegetables and fresh spinach, and mix until blended. Pour the mixture into the pie crust. Bake for 45 minutes or until the center is done. Remove from oven and allow to rest for 5 minutes before slicing. Serves 6.

# VEGETABLE SHEPHERD'S PIE

*Here's another tasty recipe I got from Tally. She manages to stay model-thin despite her love of chocolate. Maybe it's because she eats a lot of vegetables. That's a tough act for me to follow at home since Dalton is a meat and potatoes fan.*

## Ingredients

12 oz. low sodium vegetable broth
$1/3$ cup dry red wine
6 oz. can tomato paste
1 Tbsp. all-purpose flour
3 Tbsp. unsalted butter
2 lbs. sliced mushrooms
3 Tbsp. olive oil
8 oz. container chopped fresh onions
12 oz. chopped fresh celery
5 medium garlic cloves, chopped
1 medium turnip, peeled and diced
8 oz. crinkle cut carrots, halved
2 medium parsnips, peeled and diced
1 Tbsp. chopped fresh sage leaves
1 Tbsp. chopped fresh thyme leaves
6.5 oz. package peeled pearl onions
1 Tbsp. Worcestershire sauce
24 oz. package prepared garlic mashed potatoes
Paprika

## Directions

Preheat oven to 350 degrees. In a medium bowl, whisk together vegetable broth, red wine, tomato paste, and flour until blended. Set aside. Meanwhile, melt 2 Tbsp. butter in Dutch oven over medium-high heat. Add the mushrooms and 2 Tbsp. olive oil and cook until mushrooms are lightly browned. Transfer mushrooms to bowl. Add remaining butter and olive oil to pan along with onions, celery, and garlic.

Sauté vegetables 2 to 5 minutes until soft and golden. Add turnip, carrots, parsnips, herbs, pearl onions, and Worcestershire sauce. Cook until vegetables are softened. Add wine mixture to pan and deglaze by scraping up any browned bits. Stir in reserved mushrooms. Remove from heat and transfer vegetable mixture to a greased 9x13x2 inch baking dish.

Prepare potatoes according to package directions. Spread potatoes on top of vegetables. Sprinkle with paprika. Bake until top is golden and mixture is bubbly, about 20 minutes. Serves 6 to 8.

# VEGETARIAN STEW

*This stew is great to serve by itself or as an accompaniment to a chicken or fish entrée. Sometimes I'll make the latter for Brianna and Dalton, and I'll eat this alone with a salad. Add any fresh vegetables you have in stock if desired or substitute your favorites for items below. You could also serve this stew with cooked rice for a heartier meal.*

### Ingredients

2 Tbsp. olive oil
1 large onion, peeled and sliced
1 large eggplant, peeled and diced
2 large zucchini, peeled and sliced in rounds
$^1/_2$ cup water
8 oz. can reduced sodium tomato sauce
14.5 oz. can reduced sodium diced tomatoes
2 tsp. chopped garlic
16 oz. can chickpeas
$^1/_2$ tsp. allspice
$^1/_4$ cup chopped fresh parsley

### Directions

In a large skillet or soup pot, sauté onion in olive oil until starting to brown. Add eggplant. Reduce heat, cover, and cook for 5 minutes. Stir occasionally. Add zucchini, cover and cook for 3 minutes more. Add remaining ingredients. Cover and simmer for 25 minutes. Serves 4.

Nancy J. Cohen

# ZUCCHINI BISCUIT BAKE

*Here's another easy brunch dish. It makes a nice presentation at the dining table. I made this for breakfast when Brianna had a sleepover party, and it was a hit with her friends.*

## Ingredients

1 cup biscuit mix
$1/_2$ cup grated Parmesan cheese
$1/_2$ cup vegetable oil
1 Tbsp. chopped fresh dill
6 eggs, beaten
32 oz. sliced zucchini
8 oz. chopped onions
4 oz. chopped tomatoes

## Directions

Preheat oven to 375 degrees. Combine all ingredients except tomatoes in a large bowl. Pour into greased 9x13x2 inch baking dish. Sprinkle tomatoes on top. Bake for 30 minutes or until golden brown. Serves 4 to 6.

# ZUCCHINI EGG BAKE

*Zucchini lovers will enjoy this one. My Cousin Joan's husband planted tomatoes, zucchinis, and corn one summer in his backyard Massachusetts garden, and they had a bounty of produce as a result. Joan had to create some new recipes to use the veggies. After she made this for a family brunch, I requested the instructions. I'll cheat and use store-bought sliced zucchini, but if you prefer, you can use 2 large fresh zucchini, peeled and sliced in rounds.*

## Ingredients

2 Tbsp. olive oil
8 oz. diced onion
15 oz. can sweet corn, drained
(2) 16 oz. containers sliced zucchini
8 oz. diced tomatoes
8 oz. sliced mushrooms
1 Tbsp. chopped fresh basil
1 tsp. dried oregano
12 oz. shredded mozzarella cheese
6 eggs, beaten

## Directions

Preheat oven to 375 degrees. Heat the olive oil in a large skillet. Add the vegetables and sauté until softened. Remove from heat and stir in seasonings, about $2/3$ of the cheese, and the eggs. Mix thoroughly. Transfer to greased 9x13x2 inch baking dish. Sprinkle remaining cheese on top. Cover with foil and bake for 20 minutes. Remove foil and bake 10 minutes more or until browned and bubbly. Serves 4 to 6.

# ZUCCHINI QUICHE

*This recipe is handy to bake in disposable pie plates to bring to a pot-luck luncheon. Or serve one for a light meal at home and freeze the other quiche for later.*

## Ingredients

1 large onion, chopped
$1/_2$ cup vegetable oil
$1/_2$ cup grated Parmesan cheese
4 eggs, beaten
1 Tbsp. chopped fresh parsley
3 cups zucchini, peeled and grated
1 cup biscuit mix
4 oz. shredded cheddar cheese
$1/_4$ cup egg substitute

## Directions

Preheat oven to 350 degrees. Mix together the first five ingredients in a large bowl. Add the zucchini, biscuit mix, cheddar cheese, and egg substitute. Stir to blend. Spray two 9-inch pie dishes with cooking spray. Pour mixture into pie plates, dividing evenly. Bake for 40 minutes or until golden brown and center is cooked through. Serves 6.

# HAIRBALL HIJINKS

## Bad Hair Day Mystery 14.5

**The Recipes**
Chicken Orzo
Chocolate Zucchini Cake
Eggplant Tomato Casserole
Roasted Red Potatoes
Shrimp Brown Rice

*Although these recipes aren't mentioned in the tale but are offered at the end of the story, Marla finds time to have coffee with her friend, Tally. People often socialize around food and drinks, which is especially important in a mystery for interviewing suspects or counteracting the taint of murder.*

**The Story**
When hairstylist Marla Vail agrees to help find a neighbor's missing cat, she doesn't expect to get tangled in a series of home burglaries. She gets on the trail of the lost feline, surprised to find more than the pet missing from the elderly woman's house. The lady's valuables are gone, and according to the police, it isn't the first incident in the neighborhood. Can Marla outwit the crooks before they cause another cat'astrophe?

**Excerpt from Hairball Hijinks**

"I've put Luke down for a nap," Tally said. "He may be too excited to sleep, but we'll have a few minutes. Would you like a cup of coffee? I went food shopping this morning and bought some chocolate chip cookies if you want one."

"Still the chocolate addict, are you?" Marla's throat constricted. She'd feared her friend might never be the same. Thank the Lord for giving Tally back her life.

"I need to satisfy my sweet tooth," Tally replied. "Maybe it'll give me some energy. I get tired so quickly."

"That's to be expected after the ordeal you've been through. You'll regain your strength. The housekeeper I hired will be arriving soon. She'll fix your dinner while you tend to Luke. Dalton has vetted her, so her credentials check out. Do you want me to stay until she comes?"

"No, thanks. You've done so much already. I don't want to take up too much of your time." Tally poured her a cup of coffee from the coffeemaker carafe and put a carton of cream on the table. "It seems so odd here without Ken. I can't believe he isn't coming home."

"When you're ready, Dalton can help you sort through his things if you wish. But take one step at a time, or you'll feel overwhelmed."

Marla should write down a list of all the items she and Dalton had accomplished in Tally's absence. They'd already taken care of insurance, credit cards, and billing. But Tally would have to contact those companies so their correspondence reverted back to her address. And she'd need to switch the household accounts into her name. But these matters could wait until later.

"Thanks for keeping up with the mail," Tally said as though reading her mind. "That's a chore in itself."

"Everything will get done. Remember that Dalton and I are available whenever you need us."

"I know, and I love you. You're like a sister to me." Tally hugged her before they broke apart and took seats at the kitchen table.

Marla took a sip of coffee to ease her tight throat. An inner glow filled her. She had her friend back. Together, they'd face whatever life threw at them next.

Unfortunately, life threw a curveball their way before Marla could even finish her drink. A loud knock sounded in the foyer.

Hearing Luke begin to wail, she stood. "I'll get it. You take care of the baby," she told Tally. Marla hastened to the front door. After a glance through the peephole, she opened the door to face an elderly woman with white hair.

"I heard you were taking care of Tally's affairs after her accident, and I recognized your car in the driveway. You have to help me," said the lady with a frantic expression.

"I'm sorry, but I don't believe we've met."

"I'm one of Tally's neighbors. I understand you've a reputation for solving crimes. Thanks to your efforts, the police discovered who hurt Tally and her husband. Poor thing to lose her man that way. Now my guy is missing. I can't find Mr. Stanton anywhere."

"What do you mean?" Did the woman really address her spouse in that formal manner?

"I went out on some errands. When I got back, he was gone. I don't know how he could have slipped out of the house on his own."

Marla gave her a sharp glance. She wanted to learn more, but Luke had quieted, and she didn't dare risk waking the baby by asking this person inside. Besides, it wasn't her house. She didn't have that right.

However, Marla couldn't turn the woman away. Her natural inclination was to help people, so she stepped outside and shut the door behind her. The first order of business was to determine if this lady was legit or a scam artist preying on folks in the community.

## ORDER NOW at
https://nancyjcohen.com/hairball-hijinks/

# SIDE DISHES

# BARLEY CORN SALAD

*Here's a colorful, cold salad for you to offer at a buffet. You can make it ahead and refrigerate it until the party starts. If you have leftovers, serve it as a side dish with your next dinner. This was my Aunt Selma's creation. She's a fan of any food with barley.*

## Ingredients

4 cups cooked barley
32 oz. frozen corn, thawed
1 cup chopped red bell pepper
1 cup chopped green bell pepper
6 green onions, chopped
2 Tbsp. minced fresh parsley
4 Tbsp. lemon juice
4 Tbsp. canola oil
1 tsp. thyme

## Directions

Mix first 6 ingredients in a large bowl. Add lemon juice, oil, and thyme. Stir and refrigerate until served. Makes 6 to 8 servings, or more if served at a buffet where everyone only takes a spoonful.

# BARLEY PILAF

*Dalton could eat potatoes with every meal, but not me. I like this alternative with healthy grains and chopped vegetables.*

## Ingredients

1 Tbsp. butter
1 large zucchini, peeled and chopped
1 large carrot, chopped
6 oz. sliced mushrooms
8 oz. chopped onions
2 cups low sodium chicken broth
1 cup barley
$\frac{1}{2}$ tsp. dried marjoram

## Directions

Sauté zucchini, carrot, mushrooms, and onions in butter until wilted. Add broth, barley, and marjoram. Bring to a boil. Cover and lower heat to simmer until fluid is nearly absorbed. Remove from heat and let stand before serving. Add salt to taste. Optional: Add ¼ tsp. thyme, fresh chopped parsley, or another herb of choice for more flavor. Serves 4 to 6.

## BROCCOLI CHEESE BAKE

*My mother used to make this recipe for our family Thanksgiving feasts, but now she likes to do less work and brings desserts. I've inherited this dish as my favorite contribution to bring when we're not hosting at our house. I have to tell you about an incident with my poodle, Spooks. I'd made a double batch of this recipe, two half steamer trays, and left them on the kitchen table to cool before covering them with aluminum foil. I went into my home office to check my email, and when I returned, half of one steamer tray was empty! A big gouge was left in its place. There was only one creature in the house who could have jumped on the chair and stuck his snout in there. Spooks had a telltale smudge around his mouth. He ran under the table when I spotted him. Naughty dog! Thereafter, I was careful not to leave any open foods where he could reach them.*

### Ingredients

8 servings
$^1/_4$ cup chopped onions
4 Tbsp. butter
$^1/_2$ cup water
2 Tbsp. flour
8 oz. jar Cheese Whiz
(2) 10 oz. packages frozen chopped broccoli, defrosted and
    drained
$^3/_4$ cup egg substitute
$^1/_2$ cup dry bread crumbs

For $^1/_2$ steamer size (24 servings)
2 cups chopped onions
8 Tbsp. butter (1 stick)
2 cups water

8 Tbsp. flour
(2) 16 oz. jars Cheese Whiz
(4) 16 oz. packages frozen chopped broccoli, defrosted and
    drained
3 cups egg substitute
$1/_2$ cup dry bread crumbs

For full steamer size (48 servings)
4 cups chopped onions
16 Tbsp. butter (2 sticks)
4 cups water
16 Tbsp. flour
(4) 16 oz. jars Cheese Whiz
(8) 16 oz. packages frozen chopped broccoli, defrosted and
    drained
6 cups egg substitute
1 cup dry bread crumbs

**Directions**

Preheat oven to 325 degrees. Sauté onions in butter until
translucent. Mix flour in water in separate cup. Stir flour
mixture into onions and cook until thickened and boiling.
Lower heat, add Cheese Whiz, stir until it melts, then add
broccoli and egg substitute. Mix to blend.

Place mixture in a greased 9-inch square baking dish for a
smaller portion, or use half steamer trays for a larger crowd. If
you have overflow, add an additional baking dish. Sprinkle
bread crumbs on top. Bake for 45 minutes or until fully set all
the way through and browned.

If dish is not needed until later, cool and refrigerate, covered,
then reheat in the oven when the time comes. Or, this recipe
may be assembled the day before your event and baked when
preparing the meal to serve.

# CARIBBEAN RICE WITH PIGEON PEAS

*My mother once had a Jamaican housekeeper, and this woman was a fantastic cook. I coaxed her into giving us her family recipe for this rice dish. It reminds me of my cruise with Dalton on the Tropical Sun. I included this recipe in* Killer Knots *so you could recreate a touch of the Caribbean in your own kitchen.*

## Ingredients

2 cups long grain rice
13.5 oz. can coconut milk
1 cup chopped green onions
15.5 oz. can Goya dry pigeon peas (find near the canned beans)
2 Tbsp. butter
Salt to taste

## Directions

Drain and rinse peas, saving juice. Combine coconut milk, juice from peas, and enough water to make 4 cups of liquid. Pour into saucepan. Add rice and simmer covered, stirring occasionally, until most of the liquid is absorbed. Mix in green onions, pigeon peas, and butter. Add salt to taste. Serves 6 to 8.

# CAULIFLOWER COUSCOUS

*This is a great vegetable substitute for a starch. Tally gave me this recipe after she saw it on a cooking show. You'll feel healthier eating it than you would with a mouthful of mashed potatoes. Look for cauliflower rice in the fresh produce section of your supermarket. If you can't find it, buy a whole cauliflower and grind it in your food processor.*

## Ingredients

$1/_2$ cup dried apricots, cut into quarters
1 lb. cauliflower rice
2 Tbsp. butter
2 Tbsp. olive oil
1 medium onion, sliced
2 cloves garlic, minced
$1/_2$ package fresh baby spinach
15.5 oz. can garbanzo beans (chickpeas), drained and rinsed
$1/_2$ cup walnuts, chopped
$1/_2$ cup green onions, sliced

## Directions

Put the apricots into a small bowl and cover with boiling water for at least 10 minutes to soften. Drain before using. In a large pot, heat 1Tbsp. olive oil and 1Tbsp. butter. Add onion and cook until translucent. Add garlic and stir. Add cauliflower rice and cook for several minutes, stirring occasionally. Mix in apricots, spinach, chickpeas, chopped walnuts, and green onions. Stir in remaining olive oil and butter. Serve hot. Makes 4 to 6 servings.

# CHEESY HASH BROWN CASSEROLE

*Forget the low cholesterol diet if you make this dish. Dalton likes a hearty breakfast, and this recipe suits his stomach along with a helping of scrambled eggs. It's also a good brunch dish.*

## Ingredients

15 oz. can cream of celery soup
1 cup reduced fat sour cream
1 Tbsp. flour
$1/_2$ tsp. garlic powder
24 to 30 oz. package frozen hash brown potatoes
2 cups reduced fat shredded cheddar cheese
$1/_3$ cup grated Parmesan cheese
Paprika to taste

## Directions

Preheat oven to 350 degrees. In a bowl, combine soup, sour cream, flour, and garlic powder. Stir in potatoes and cheddar cheese. Pour into a greased 9x13x2 inch baking dish. Sprinkle Parmesan cheese and paprika on top. Bake uncovered for 50 to 60 minutes or until browned and bubbly. Serves 6 to 8.

Nancy J. Cohen

# CURRIED RICE AND PEAS

*Curry gives this recipe an extra zing. It makes a colorful party salad or a hot side dish that pairs well with chicken. Consider adding some diced pimento or chopped red bell pepper for added color.*

## Ingredients

4 cups water
2 cups uncooked long grain rice
1 Tbsp. butter
16 oz. package frozen peas, thawed
1 cup diced celery
5 green onions, sliced
$1/_2$ cup mayonnaise
$1/_2$ cup apricot jam
$1^1/_2$ tsp. curry powder
1 sprinkle turmeric

## Directions

Combine water, rice and butter in a saucepan and bring to a boil. Reduce heat and simmer, stirring occasionally, until water is absorbed. Remove from heat and mix in peas, celery, and green onions. In a separate bowl, blend mayonnaise, apricot jam, curry powder, and turmeric. Add to rice mixture and mix well. May be served warm or chilled. Makes 6 to 8 servings.

# GINGERED BRUSSEL SPROUTS

*Now that you can buy shaved Brussel sprouts at the supermarket, this dish is a breeze to make. It's healthy and satisfying as a side dish to go along with your choice of protein.*

## Ingredients

10 oz. package shaved Brussel sprouts
1 Tbsp. olive oil
8 oz. chopped onions
1 Tbsp. minced fresh, peeled ginger
1 tsp. minced garlic
2 Tbsp. water

## Directions

In a large skillet over medium-high heat, sauté Brussel sprouts in olive oil until wilted. Stir in onions, ginger and garlic. Add water. Reduce heat to medium and cook covered for 15 minutes or until vegetables are tender.

# GLAZED SWEET POTATOES

*This variation on the usual mashed sweet potatoes makes for an enticing presentation and stretches more than if you made a simple baked sweet potato. Try it with your Thanksgiving turkey or with any poultry dish. My brother, Michael, isn't fond of marshmallows. If I feel ambitious, I'll make this recipe just for him at holiday dinners when I'm hosting.*

## Ingredients

3 large sweet potatoes
$1/_3$ cup granulated sugar
$1/_3$ cup dark brown sugar
$3/_4$ cup water
2 Tbsp. butter
3 Tbsp. lemon juice
$1/_2$ tsp. freshly grated nutmeg
$1/_4$ tsp. cinnamon

## Directions

Preheat oven to 350 degrees. Simmer potatoes in pot of boiling water for about 10 minutes. Drain and cool. Peel potatoes and slice crosswise into ¾ inch slices.

In a separate small saucepan, blend granulated and dark brown sugars and ¾ cup water. Bring to a boil, stirring until sugars are dissolved. Simmer on low heat for 8 minutes and then remove from heat. Whisk in butter, lemon juice, nutmeg, and cinnamon.

Arrange potatoes in single layer on greased 9x13x2 inch baking pan. Drizzle lemon syrup over potatoes. Bake for 40 to 50 minutes, turning over halfway, until fork-tender. Serves 6 to 8.

# GREEN BEAN CASSEROLE

*If you're diet-conscious, use the healthier choice soups for this recipe. It's easy to make if you buy frozen green beans. This dish is a staple at our Thanksgiving dinners.*

## Ingredients

(2) 10.5 oz. cans cream of mushroom soup
1 cup reduced fat milk
2 tsp. low sodium soy sauce
(2) 32 oz. bags frozen French-cut green beans, cooked and drained
6 oz. can fried onions

## Directions

Preheat oven to 350 degrees. Mix together the soup, milk, soy sauce, green beans, and half the onions in a greased casserole dish. Bake for 25 minutes or until bubbly. Top with remaining onions and bake for 5 minutes more or until onions are browned. Makes 12 servings. Optional: Substitute Worcestershire sauce for soy sauce.

# ISRAELI COUSCOUS WITH MUSHROOMS

*Large-grained couscous works well in this dish with assorted mushrooms. While I don't add salt to my recipes, you can add seasoning to suit your palate. This makes an enticing side dish to accompany any type of protein. I like to pair it with a savory beef brisket as a substitute for starchy potatoes.*

## Ingredients

2 cups large-grained couscous
Low sodium chicken broth
8 oz. fresh gourmet mushroom blend, coarsely chopped
2 garlic cloves, peeled and chopped
2 Tbsp. olive oil
1 tsp. fresh thyme
1 Tbsp. Worcestershire sauce

## Directions

Preheat oven to 400 degrees. Cook couscous in chicken broth according to package directions. Transfer to serving dish, cover, and set aside.

Mix together mushrooms, garlic, olive oil, and thyme, and spread on greased aluminum foil-lined 9x13x2 inch baking pan. Bake for 20 minutes. Add mushroom mixture to cooked couscous, stir in Worcestershire sauce, and mix to blend. Serves 6 to 8.

# MUSHROOM RISOTTO

*Instead of plain rice to go with a meal, try this mushroom risotto. But don't make the mistake that Dalton did. He was making dinner to surprise me, and he thought risotto rice was similar to quick-cooking rice. Forget reading the directions. He neglected to add liquid at regular intervals and cook the rice slowly as required. When I bit into a hard grain of rice during dinner, I suspected he hadn't cooked it long enough. I was right, so educate your sous chefs about the different varieties of rice. Regarding the chicken broth, I use it at room temperature, but you can heat it slightly in the microwave if you wish to keep it warm during the cooking process.*

## Ingredients

3 Tbsp. olive oil
1$1/2$ pounds sliced fresh mushrooms
$1/2$ cup port wine
48 oz. chicken broth
2 cups chopped onions
2 cups Arborio rice
1 cup dry white wine
1 cup freshly grated Parmesan cheese

## Directions

In a sauté pan, heat 1Tbsp. olive oil. Add the mushrooms and stir until softened. Add the port wine and $1/2$ cup chicken broth, and simmer for 5 minutes. Remove from heat.

In a heavy duty soup pot, heat 2 Tbsp. olive oil. Add the onions and sauté until lightly browned, then add the rice and toss until rice turns golden. Add white wine and simmer until most of the wine has been absorbed. Then add the chicken broth, one cup at a time. Simmer until stock has been absorbed then add more broth.

After the final cup of broth, add the mushroom mixture, stir, and continue to cook until most of the liquid is gone. Stir in the Parmesan cheese and serve hot. Serves 4 to 6.

# NOODLE KUGEL

*This classic Jewish recipe has many variations, but this is the one I inherited from my mother. You'll surprise your dinner guests if you serve this as a side dish for a change of pace. Or serve it to accompany roast chicken for a traditional meal.*

## Ingredients

16 oz. bag wide egg noodles
4 eggs, beaten
$1/2$ cup sugar
$1/2$ pound butter, melted
$1/4$ tsp. cinnamon
20 oz. can crushed pineapple, drained
Juice from 1 lemon
Cornflake crumbs
Cinnamon sugar

## Directions

Preheat oven to 350 degrees. Cook the noodles in boiling water for 8 minutes, then drain and rinse under cold water. Stir a few noodles into the beaten eggs. Pour eggs into bowl with noodles and mix. Add sugar, melted butter, cinnamon, drained pineapple, and lemon juice. Stir until blended. Pour into a greased 9x13x2 inch baking pan. Sprinkle cornflake crumbs and cinnamon sugar on top. Bake for 50 minutes or until browned and bubbly. Optional: Cut butter to ¼ pound and add one pint sour cream; Add one tsp. vanilla instead of lemon juice; or Add $1/2$ cup golden raisins.

# POTATO ONION BAKE

*This lip-smacking recipe is easy to make and suitable for a dinner party or brunch. Potatoes always pair well with onions and garlic. If you have a mandolin, use it to slice the potatoes.*

## Ingredients

2 pounds Yukon gold potatoes, peeled and thinly sliced
2 Tbsp. olive oil
2 large onions, peeled and sliced
2 tsp. chopped garlic
1 tsp. dried thyme
1 Tbsp. chopped fresh rosemary
14.5 oz. can low sodium chicken broth

## Directions

Preheat oven to 400 degrees. Heat olive oil in large skillet. Sauté onions and garlic until onions are translucent. Stir in thyme and rosemary. Layer potatoes and onion mixture in a greased 9x13x2 inch baking dish. Pour broth over all. Cover dish with foil. Bake for 30 minutes. Uncover and bake until potatoes are tender and browned, about 15 minutes more. Serves 6 to 8.

# POTATO ZUCCHINI MASH

*Here's another recipe for your brunch or dinner side. You'll be getting your veggies and starch all in one in this hearty dish.*

## Ingredients

30 oz. package frozen shredded hash brown potatoes
10 oz. package matchstick carrots
3 large zucchini, peeled and shredded
5 eggs
$3/4$ cup mayonnaise
$1/4$ cup fresh chopped onions
2 Tbsp. chopped garlic
3 Tbsp. egg substitute

## Directions

Preheat oven to 350 degrees. In a large bowl, combine potatoes, carrots, and zucchini. In a separate small bowl, beat the eggs. Add mayonnaise and onions. Stir egg mixture into potatoes. Add chopped garlic and egg substitute. Blend until moist. Transfer into greased 9x13x2 inch baking dish. Bake, uncovered, for 1 hour, or until edges are browned. Serves 6 to 8.

# RICE WITH PEAS AND GARLIC

*If you feel like enhancing your rice with more taste and color, this is the recipe for you. It's easy peasy to make (pun intended).*

## Ingredients

$1/_4$ pound butter
16 oz. chopped onions
8 oz. chopped green onions
3 Tbsp. chopped garlic
3 cups uncooked long grain rice
5 cups reduced sodium chicken broth
1 bag frozen green peas, thawed
1 Tbsp. olive oil
Salt to taste

## Directions

Melt butter in large saucepan. Add onions and garlic and sauté until wilted. Mix in rice and stir until coated and starting to brown. Pour in broth and bring to a boil. Reduce heat and simmer, covered, until liquid is nearly absorbed. Add green peas and cook until heated through. Stir in olive oil. Add salt to taste. Serves 8 to 10.

# ROASTED ACORN SQUASH

*My stepdaughter, Brianna, loves this simple side dish seasoned with herbs of your choice or the ones listed below. It beats my usual method of cooking a squash in the microwave, halving it and removing the seeds, then melting brown sugar in the hollow. This variation cuts the calories.*

## Ingredients

2 Acorn Squash
Olive Oil
Paprika, Oregano, Parsley, Garlic Powder

## Directions

Preheat oven to 350 degrees. Cook acorn squash in microwave on high for a few minutes until somewhat soft. Place the squash on a cutting board and slice it in half length-wise. Remove the seeds. Lay the half pieces cut-side-down on the board and slice into ¼ inch length-wise slices or along ridges.

Arrange the slices in a single layer on a greased aluminum-foil lined baking sheet. Drizzle olive oil over the top of each squash piece and sprinkle with spices. Bake for 40 to 50 minutes or until slices are fork-tender. Serves 4.

# ROASTED CAULIFLOWER

*Cousin Cynthia served this at Rosh Hashanah dinner one year when she hosted, and I was hooked on the easy and yet healthful recipe. It truly tastes more delicious than it sounds.*

## Ingredients

1 head cauliflower, broken into florets
2 Tbsp. olive oil
$1\frac{1}{2}$ tsp. paprika

## Directions

Preheat oven to 400 degrees. Line a baking sheet with aluminum foil and coat with cooking spray. Spread cauliflower on foil. Sprinkle with olive oil and paprika. Bake for 30 minutes or until tender and lightly browned. Serves 4.

# ROSEMARY RED POTATOES

*This recipe is easy to make and goes well with any source of protein. If you want to make it even easier, buy pre-sliced onions. You can double the recipe for a larger crowd.*

## Ingredients

3 lb. bag of petite red potatoes
1 Tbsp. fresh chopped garlic
1 large onion, sliced
0.75 oz. package fresh rosemary, stemmed and chopped
Olive Oil

## Directions

Preheat oven to 400 degrees. Clean half of potatoes and cut into quarters. Store the rest for another use. Put the cut potatoes into a large bowl. Mix in garlic, onions and rosemary. Add enough olive oil to moisten. Spread onto greased 9x13x2 inch baking sheet. Bake on the next up-from-bottom rack for 30 to 45 minutes or until potatoes are browned and fork-tender. Serves 4.

# SPINACH MUSHROOM CASSEROLE

*Would you like to serve a side dish for company that isn't the same standard fare? Whip up this recipe and surprise everyone. I had it at a pot-luck dinner at a friend's house one night when I was still married to Stan. It's not something I make often, but my guests are pleased when I do. The curry gives it an unexpected flavor.*

## Ingredients

(2) 10 oz. packages frozen chopped spinach
8 oz. can tomato sauce
2 cups grated cheddar cheese
2 cups sour cream
(2) 4.5 oz. jars sliced mushrooms
$1/_2$ tsp. curry powder
Dash of freshly grated nutmeg

## Directions

Preheat oven to 350 degrees. Cook spinach according to package instructions. Drain liquid and squeeze dry. In a bowl, mix spinach and remaining ingredients. Put into a greased 2-quart casserole dish. Bake for 30 minutes. Serves 6.

# SPINACH NOODLE SURPRISE

*My friend Tally came up with the idea of using almond milk in this recipe when she was pregnant with Luke. She wasn't fond of regular milk but needed to get her calcium intake. The cheese helped in that regard, too. I like this dish enough that I could make it a main meal.*

## Ingredients

8 oz. package spinach fettuccini
10.5 oz can cream of mushroom soup
5 oz. milk or unsweetened almond milk
7 oz. package sliced Swiss cheese
$1/_2$ cup dry bread crumbs

## Directions

Preheat oven to 400 degrees. Cook noodles according to package directions. Drain and put into a large bowl. In a smaller bowl, whisk together the soup and milk until blended. Pour into larger bowl with noodles. Transfer mixture to a greased 2-quart baking dish. Place cheese slices on top and sprinkle with bread crumbs. Bake for 20 minutes or until browned and bubbly. Serves 6 to 8.

# SWEET POTATOES WITH MARSHMALLOWS

*This standard Thanksgiving accompaniment wouldn't be the same without marshmallows. I have to hide the bag in the pantry or Dalton will snack on them. He'll pop them in his mouth like candy. Be careful to watch the topping carefully in the oven so it doesn't burn.*

## Ingredients

(2) 40-oz. cans sweet potatoes or yams
$1/_2$ cup unsalted butter, melted
$1/_2$ cup light corn syrup
1 bag mini marshmallows

## Directions

Preheat oven to 350 degrees. Drain and mash potatoes. Stir in melted butter and corn syrup. Put into greased 9x13x2 inch baking dish. Sprinkle marshmallows on top and bake until marshmallows are browned and bubbly. Options: Add a 20 oz. can of drained crushed pineapple to potato mixture. Or substitute maple syrup for corn syrup. For a larger crowd, add extra cans of yams. Serves 8 to 10.

# SWEET POTATOES WITH RED ONIONS AND ROSEMARY

*This is a healthier way to serve sweet potatoes and makes a good side dish to meat, poultry or fish. Dalton is happy when I serve any kind of potatoes with his meal.*

## Ingredients

3 large sweet potatoes, peeled
8 Tbsp. canola oil
3 tsp. minced garlic
2 large red onions, peeled
2 Tbsp. chopped fresh rosemary
$1/4$ cup grated Parmesan cheese

## Directions

Preheat oven to 375 degrees. Cut potatoes lengthwise and then into one inch cubes. Mix with 6 Tbsp. oil and minced garlic. Spread on greased, foil-lined baking sheet. Meanwhile, cut onions lengthwise and then crosswise into chunks. Mix with remaining 2 Tbsp. oil and spread on another greased, foil-lined baking sheet.

Put potatoes on center rack and onions on bottom rack. Roast for 30 minutes. Halfway through, turn both batches and sprinkle rosemary on potatoes. When both vegetables are tender, remove from oven and toss together in a bowl. Sprinkle cheese into mixture before serving. Serves 4 to 6.

Nancy J. Cohen

# WILD RICE, BARLEY, & MUSHROOM CASSEROLE

*My mother makes this recipe to accompany a tender brisket. I like the slightly nutty texture. It seems less caloric than potatoes and with healthier grains. Plus, it's an easy-to-prepare microwavable recipe. This has become one of my favorite go-to company side dishes.*

## Ingredients

$1/_2$ cup unsalted butter
1 medium onion, chopped
8 oz. wild rice
2 Tbsp. pearl barley
28 oz. beef broth
$1/_4$ tsp. dried thyme
8 oz. sliced mushrooms

## Directions

Melt ¼ cup butter in 2 quart microwave casserole on high. Add onion and cook uncovered on high until soft, about 1 minute. Add rice, barley, beef broth, and thyme. Cover tightly and cook on high for 25 minutes. Stir and cook on medium setting for about 40 minutes, or until most liquid is absorbed.

Melt remaining ¼ cup butter in shallow 10 inch microwave dish on high. Add mushrooms. Cook uncovered on high until mushrooms are tender, about 4 to 5 minutes. Stir mushrooms into cooked rice and barley mixture. Serves 6.

# KILLER KNOTS

## Bad Hair Day Mystery #9

**The Recipes**
> Caribbean Rice with Pigeon Peas
> Island Turkey Thighs
> Apple Ginger Cake

**The Story**
Florida hairstylist Marla Shore hopes for a romantic interlude with her fiancé on a Caribbean cruise, but troubled waters lie ahead when their dinner companions disappear one-by-one. Then Marla learns a killer is along for the ride. Onboard art auctions, ports of call, and sumptuous buffets beckon, but she ignores temptation and musters her sleuthing skills to expose the culprit. She'd better find him fast, before her next shore excursion turns into a trip to Davy Jones's locker.

**Nancy's Comments**
Call it a Caribbean Night when you make these recipes and add a mixed rum drink to the menu. Some of the best food-related activities we've done on cruises have been on Dominica, Puerto Rico, and Grenada. This doesn't count the rum distillery tour on St. Croix.

Grenada is the Spice Island, and as you drive around, you see nutmeg hanging from trees and other exotic fruits and spices among the lush tropical growth. It's a good place to stock your own spice shelf as well as to pick up some packaged gifts. We enjoyed a tour through a botanical garden where the guide pointed out the various plants and their uses for food or medicine.

Foodie tours are one of my favorite activities on cruises. In San Juan, we climbed the hilly city streets, stopping at a café along the way to taste their strong coffee along with a soft pastry covered with powdered sugar. From here we went to a restaurant where our group sat outdoors at a long table. We made our own Mojito cocktails. (Add 4 to 5 mint leaves to a glass and crush with pestle. Add a spoonful of natural or light brown sugar. Use pestle to blend. Pour in 1 shot of rum. Add club soda.) Using a thicker pestle, we ground up fried plantains then added shredded (pulled) cooked chicken with Creole sauce. This was our main dish, served with rice and red beans. For dessert, we headed to another restaurant for a flan that tasted more like cheesecake.

In Dominica, we signed up for a cooking class that took place at a mountain estate with wonderful scenic views. Here we donned aprons and pitched in to make Creole fish, rice and peas in coconut milk, plantains in shredded coconut, a pumpkin drink called Wicked Jack, and grapefruit with rum liqueur. And while dining at Senor Frog's in Nassau, I picked up a good recipe for guacamole from watching the waiter prepare it at our table. You can see pictures from these tours and more to come on my Facebook Page.

## Excerpt from Killer Knots

Marla had just crossed the road when a flash of movement caught her eye. Entering the Guavaberry Mercantile farther down Front Street was an older woman with teased blond hair, a heavy application of makeup, and a silk blouse and skirt. She looked too elegant for an ordinary tourist and too well dressed for a native. Wondering if this could be the elusive countess, Marla hurried after her. Charmed by the cherry-red cottage with gingerbread trim, Marla entered the emporium. Inside to the left stretched a mahogany bar topped with liquor bottles and disposable plastic cups.

"Hello, missy," said the bartender, a large-girthed dark woman with a singsong voice. Her brilliant smile revealed yellowed teeth. She wore a turban, the fabric matching her flowery caftan. "Would you like to sample our famous island guavaberry drink?"

Marla glanced to her right, where shelves stocked with hot sauces, cookbooks, boxed rum cakes, and souvenir glassware took up space. Beyond the front section, which may have been the living-room space of a converted house, sat a cloth-draped round table with two chairs. A beaded curtain separated the rest of the place from the public. The strips of beads wavered, as though someone had just passed through.

"Where's the woman who just came in here?" Marla asked. Behind her, she heard a bell tinkle over the door as another patron entered.

The bartender's gaze flickered momentarily with recognition. "She went back to prepare for a reading. You got business with the countess? I'll give you a drink while you wait. You taste this, you wanna buy."

Marla shifted her purse, watching the man who'd come in from the corner of her eye. He wore a black T-shirt and baggy pants and had the swarthy complexion of a native. Her skin prickled. He appeared to be browsing the gift items, but she'd swear his intent wasn't on shopping. Never mind him. The bartender had mentioned the countess, so she was on the right track.

"You say the countess is here for a reading? Do you tell fortunes?"

"Madame Nadine reads your signs, lady," the proprietress said in a haughty tone. "I have the gift, same as my mama before me. You want an appointment? Rules say you gotta sample my brew first. I know you'll wanna buy a bottle for your friends back home."

"Okay, fine, I'll buy a couple of bottles. Just tell the countess I need to talk to her, okay?"

"Countess Delacroix don't just talk to nobody. Why you wanna see her?"

"A friend of mine gave me her name. I have some questions to ask about a mutual acquaintance." Then, suddenly afraid she wouldn't be able to communicate with the Frenchwoman, Marla queried, "She does speak English clearly enough, doesn't she?"

The bartender laughed, a wheezy sound coming from deep within her chest. "She done speak seven languages, lady. It's all that vanilla. Makes her smart."

"Vanilla?"

"You don't know why she's so rich? True vanilla is expensive, and Countess Delacroix's family owns many plantations. See those shelves over there?" She pointed toward a row of labeled brown bottles. "I carry her product, pure Mexican vanilla extract. You go to Cozumel, and you'll find lots of bottles for sale, but it ain't always real."

Marla glanced at the man, who was busy perusing a selection of Caribbean coffees. He'd paid no heed to their discussion, but he wasn't in any hurry to make a purchase either.

Madame Nadine poured a few ounces from two different bottles into the plastic cups. "You there, mister. Come taste a free sample. You'll like this better than that other shop down the street. My prices beat theirs, too."

"Thanks, I could use a shot," he said, sauntering over.

Marla took a step back, observing his stubbled jaw and glacier eyes. "Look, I have to get back to my ship. Is the countess coming out or not? She shouldn't have to prepare for a reading. I've had one by a psychic, and Reverend Hazel held my eyeglass case for vibes." Her predictions had been right on the mark, too, but then Cassadaga, Florida was known for its certified mediums.

Feeling parched as well as frustrated, Marla snatched one of the little cups and gulped the contents. Her throat constricted as the strong liquor scorched her esophagus. Its fruity taste left a pleasant aftermath, making her consider its possibilities as a gift for her brother back home.

"Wait here," Madame Nadine told her. "I'll go get Countess Delacroix for you."

As the shopkeeper disappeared behind the curtain, Marla felt a tap on her shoulder. She spun to face the man hovering by the bar. A grin split his face like an axe cleaving a tree trunk, giving her the impression he didn't smile often.

"Try this," he said, holding up one of the little cups. "It's sweeter than the other. People from the States like it a lot better."

Marla grasped the cup, wondering what was taking Madame Nadine so long to retrieve the countess. Maybe she should have followed her through the curtain. Without thought, she downed the liquor, setting her empty vessel on the polished countertop. That should quench her thirst until she got back to their cabin.

Glancing at her watch, she winced. "I can't wait any longer. Will you tell Madame Nadine that I had to leave? I've wasted too much time here already." She was beginning to think she'd been bamboozled about Countess Delacroix even being there. Likely the woman had left through a rear exit.

*And likely Dalton will be white with worry over my absence.*

Berating herself for lingering, she hastened toward the door. Midway there, a twinge of queasiness hit her stomach. Oh great. She shouldn't have drunk alcohol on top of that meal from the French café. Or maybe the liquor didn't agree with her. Who knew what extra ingredients it contained?

Her vision tunneled as a wave of heat struck her skin and flushed her face. Were those walls moving inward, or was it the enclosed, stuffy atmosphere making her sweat?

She lurched toward the exit, stumbling as dizziness overwhelmed her.

*Go outside!* her mind shouted. She forced herself to move forward, but her feet wouldn't cooperate. She gasped as her stomach clenched with a sudden, sharp pain, and then all went black.

**ORDER NOW** at
https://nancyjcohen.com/killer-knots/

# DESSERTS

# AMARETTO CAKE

*This delicious moist cake will have guests reaching for more. You can adjust the liqueur levels to suit your taste, but vary the amount of water accordingly to keep the same proportions of liquid.*

## Ingredients

15.25 oz. box yellow cake mix
5.1 oz. box instant vanilla pudding
$1/_2$ cup Amaretto
$3/_4$ cup water
$1/_2$ cup canola oil
4 large eggs
$1/_4$ tsp. almond extract
$1/_8$ tsp. freshly grated nutmeg

## Icing

1 cup powdered sugar
3 Tbsp. Amaretto

## Directions

Preheat oven to 350 degrees. Add all ingredients into a large bowl and beat with mixer for 1 minute on low. Scrape down sides with spatula and beat for another 2 minutes on high. Pour batter into greased and floured tube pan. Bake for 45 minutes or until golden brown.

Cool on rack. Invert cake onto plate. Mix together powdered sugar in a small bowl with Amaretto. Drizzle over cake as a glaze. Slice and serve.

# APPLE GINGER CAKE

*Another friend of mine, Wendy, will only eat desserts with fruit because she says they're healthier. Considering the sugar, I wouldn't agree, but at least you'll get your fruit portion for the day. This one delights the palate with its gingerbread-like flavor. This recipe appeared in* Killer Knots. *The molasses reminds me of the sugar mills in the Caribbean where Dalton and I sailed on our first cruise. Consider adding a splash of rum for a taste of the islands.*

## Ingredients

$^2/_3$ cup light brown sugar
$^1/_3$ cup applesauce
1 large egg
3 Tbsp. unsulphured molasses
$1^1/_2$ cups all-purpose flour
1 tsp. baking powder
1 tsp. baking soda
1 tsp. cinnamon
2 tsp. ground ginger
$^1/_4$ tsp. freshly grated nutmeg
$^1/_8$ tsp. allspice
$^1/_2$ cup low fat vanilla yogurt
1 Gala apple, peeled, cored, and chopped
Whipped topping (optional)
Light or spiced rum (optional)

## Directions

Preheat oven to 350 degrees. In a large bowl, combine brown

sugar, applesauce, egg, and molasses. In separate bowl, mix flour, baking powder, baking soda, and spices. Add dry ingredients to molasses mixture alternately with yogurt, beating until well blended. Fold in apples. Pour into greased 9-inch square baking dish. Bake for 30 minutes or until toothpick comes out clean. Slice and serve warm.

Optional: Sprinkle light rum onto individual portions and serve with whipped topping. Or stir spiced rum into whipped cream and serve.

# APPLE RUM CAKE

*I like this recipe that uses an easy cake mix and prepared pie filling. When you don't have much time to spend in the kitchen, convenience matters. Whip this up to impress your dinner guests and serve with vanilla ice cream for extra pizzazz.*

## Ingredients

15.25 oz. box spice cake mix
21 oz. can apple pie filling
3 eggs
$^3/_4$ cup light sour cream
$^1/_4$ cup rum
2 Tbsp. canola oil
1 tsp. almond extract
2 Tbsp. dark brown sugar
1$^1/_2$ tsp. ground cinnamon
$^2/_3$ cup powdered sugar
2 tsp. reduced fat milk

## Directions

Preheat oven to 350 degrees. Set aside 1 Tbsp. cake mix and 1½ cups of pie filling. In a large bowl, combine eggs, sour cream, rum, canola oil, almond extract, remaining cake mix and pie filling. Beat on medium speed for 2 minutes. Pour half the batter into a greased fluted cake pan. In a separate small bowl, mix together the brown sugar, cinnamon, reserved 1 Tbsp. cake mix and pie filling. Spoon over batter. Top with remaining batter. Bake for 45 minutes.

Cool on rack. Invert cake onto plate. In a small bowl, mix powdered sugar and milk. Dribble over cake as a glaze. Slice and serve.

# BANANA CHOCOLATE CHIP LOAF

*Dalton's cousin from Arizona gave me this recipe. We tasted it when we went there on our belated honeymoon, which you can read about in* Peril by Ponytail. *This moist loaf is simple to make and is rated a winner by our family.*

## Ingredients

1 stick unsalted butter, softened
1 cup sugar
1 tsp. vanilla
2 eggs
$1^1/_2$ cup flour
1 tsp. baking powder
$^1/_2$ tsp. baking soda
4 Tbsp. sour cream
2 ripe bananas, mashed
1 cup semi-sweet chocolate chips

## Directions

Preheat oven to 350 degrees. Cream butter with sugar in a large bowl. Add vanilla, eggs, flour, baking powder, baking soda, and sour cream. Mix to blend. Add mashed bananas. Fold in chocolate chips. Put into a greased loaf pan. Bake for 1 hour or until toothpick inserted in center comes out clean. Slice and serve.

# BLUEBERRY CRUMBLE

*Here's another recipe from my friend Wendy, who goes to U-pick farms whenever she gets the chance. If you end up with an abundance of blueberries, make this quick dessert. It's delicious served warm with whipped topping or vanilla ice cream. You can use plain instant oatmeal or a flavored variety of your choice.*

## Ingredients

2 pints fresh blueberries
2 Tbsp. fresh lemon juice
$1/4$ tsp. cinnamon
$2/3$ cup sugar
$2/3$ cup flour
1 packet instant oatmeal
4 Tbsp. unsalted butter, softened
Cinnamon sugar

## Directions

Preheat oven to 350 degrees. Spread blueberries in bottom of greased 9-inch square baking dish. Sprinkle with lemon juice, cinnamon, and sugar. In a separate bowl, combine flour, contents of oatmeal packet, and softened butter. Mixture should resemble small crumbs. Spread over blueberries. Sprinkle top with cinnamon sugar. Bake for 30 minutes or until browned and bubbly. Serve warm.

# CHOCOLATE CAKE

*Tally, my best friend who's a chocoholic, created this lower calorie variation on a classic chocolate cake. She insists it's a healthier version and will keep your waistline trim. It's a way for chocolate lovers on a diet to have their cake and eat it, too.*

## Ingredients

2 egg whites
1 egg
1 $^1/_3$ cups water
8 oz. low fat plain yogurt
15.25 oz. box Devil's Food cake mix
$^1/_2$ cup unsweetened cocoa powder
2 tsp. powdered sugar

## Directions

Preheat oven to 350 degrees. In a medium bowl, combine egg whites, egg, water, and yogurt. In a large mixing bowl, blend cake mix and cocoa. Beating at low speed, add liquid mixture to dry ingredients. Blend well.

Pour batter into greased and floured fluted tube pan. Bake for 35 minutes or until toothpick inserted in center comes out clean. Cool on rack. Invert cake onto plate. Dust with powdered sugar. Slice and serve.

# CHOCOLATE MINT TORTE

*My mother has a liquor cabinet that isn't getting much use these days, so she found a recipe that included one of her flavored liqueurs. She used whipped topping for the filling, but you could try 1 cup heavy cream instead and whip it up with the liqueur and powdered sugar. If you have extra filling, serve it in a bowl on the side with the cake. I'd like to try this recipe with marshmallow cream. A small slice goes a long way for this rich dessert.*

## Ingredients

$3/4$ cup flour
$1/4$ cup unsweetened cocoa powder
1 tsp. baking powder
$1/4$ tsp. salt
3 eggs, beaten
1 cup sugar
$1/3$ cup Vandermint liqueur
Powdered sugar

## Filling
8 oz. whipped topping
2 Tbsp. Vandermint liqueur
2 Tbsp. powdered sugar

## Directions

Preheat oven to 375 degrees. Line a 10x15 inch baking pan with wax paper. Coat with cooking spray. In a medium bowl, sift together flour, cocoa powder, baking powder and salt.

Using an electric mixer, beat eggs in a large bowl until well blended. Gradually add 1 cup sugar. Mix in Vandermint liqueur. Stir in dry ingredients in batches until smooth.

Pour into baking pan and bake for 15 minutes. Invert cake onto towel sprinkled with powdered sugar and remove wax paper. Allow cake to rest. Meanwhile, blend whipped topping with 2 Tbsp. Vandermint liqueur and 2 Tbsp. powdered sugar. Cut cake into thirds cross-wise. Spread filling on top of first third. Place second cake piece on top. Cover with another layer of filling. Top with remaining third piece of cake. Sprinkle powdered sugar on top. Refrigerate until ready to serve. Slice and serve cold. Makes 8 to 10 servings.

# CHOCOLATE ZUCCHINI CAKE

*Tally came up with the idea of adding zucchini into her standard chocolate cake mixture to add moisture and nutrients at the same time. This one is a hit with Dalton who likes the idea of combining his vegetables with dessert. If you don't have buttermilk, add 1 teaspoon vinegar to $^1/_2$ cup of milk.*

## Ingredients

$2^1/_4$ cups sifted all-purpose flour
$^1/_2$ cup unsweetened cocoa powder
1 tsp. baking soda
1 tsp. salt
$1^3/_4$ cups sugar
$^1/_2$ cup unsalted butter, room temperature
$^1/_2$ cup vegetable oil
2 large eggs
1 tsp. vanilla extract
$^1/_2$ cup buttermilk
2 cups grated, unpeeled zucchini
6 oz. package semisweet chocolate chips
$^3/_4$ cup chopped walnuts

## Directions

Preheat oven to 325 degrees. Grease and flour a 9x13x2 inch baking pan. Sift the flour, cocoa, baking soda and salt together into a medium bowl. In a separate bowl, beat the sugar, softened butter, and oil until blended. Add eggs one at a time and beat well. Add vanilla, and then mix in dry ingredients alternating with buttermilk. Mix in grated zucchini.

Pour batter into prepared baking pan. Sprinkle semisweet chocolate chips and nuts on top. Bake for 50 minutes or until toothpick inserted in center comes out clean.

# COCONUT FUDGE PIE

*I made this recipe as my contest entry for the bake-off at Kinsdale Farms. That's where I discovered another contestant face-down in the strawberry field. This unfortunate incident didn't negate my affection for this dessert as it's always a crowd-pleaser. Read more about my harrowing experiences in* Trimmed to Death.

## Ingredients

3 oz. unsweetened chocolate
$1/_2$ cup unsalted butter
3 eggs, slightly beaten
$3/_4$ cup sugar
$1/_2$ cup all-purpose flour
1 tsp. vanilla
$2/_3$ cup sweetened condensed milk
$2^2/_3$ cups flaked coconut

## Directions

Preheat oven to 350 degrees. Melt chocolate and butter in a saucepan over low heat. Stir in beaten eggs, sugar, flour and vanilla. Pour into greased 9-inch pie dish. In a separate bowl, combine sweetened condensed milk and coconut. Spoon over the chocolate mixture, leaving a 1-inch border. Bake for 30 minutes. Cool on rack. Slice and serve warm.

# FRUIT COBBLER

*I ate this for the first time when I attended a dessert party with my mother at her Hadassah officer installation meeting. When I asked for the recipe, I couldn't believe how easy it was to make. You can use any fruited pie filling of your choice.*

### Ingredients

$1/_4$ cup unsalted butter
$1^1/_2$ cups biscuit mix
1 cup sugar
$2/_3$ cup reduced fat milk
21 oz. can fruit pie filling: apples, peaches, cherries, etc.
Cinnamon

### Directions

Preheat oven to 400 degrees. Melt the butter and spread it on the bottom of a 9x13x2 inch baking pan. In a bowl, whisk together the biscuit mix, sugar, and milk. Pour batter into pan. Drop the fruit to cover batter evenly. Sprinkle cinnamon on top. Bake for 30 minutes or until browned and bubbly.

# FUDGE RUM BALLS

*One year at Dalton's work Christmas party, these fudge balls were a hit. They're a great holiday recipe for the winter season or any time when you want to serve a special treat. Use whatever type of rum you prefer.*

## Ingredients

1 cup crushed vanilla wafers
1 cup powdered sugar
3 Tbsp. unsweetened cocoa powder
2 cups chopped walnuts
3 Tbsp. white corn syrup
$1/4$ cup rum
Candied cherries

## Directions

Mix together crushed vanilla wafers, powdered sugar, cocoa powder, and 1 cup chopped walnuts. Add white corn syrup and rum and mix well. Scoop mixture into 1 inch balls. Roll each ball in remaining chopped walnuts. Press one half of a candied cherry on top. Refrigerate or freeze until served. Makes about 30 balls.

# KAHLUA CHOCOLATE CAKE

*Have a slice of this sensuous cake to get your caffeine shot for the day. With coffee, chocolate, and Kahlua, you'll be well fortified and set to go. This one is always a winner.*

## Ingredients

15.25 oz. box yellow cake mix
5.1 oz. instant chocolate pudding mix
4 large eggs
$^{1}/_{2}$ cup vegetable oil
$^{3}/_{4}$ cup brewed coffee
$^{2}/_{3}$ cup Kahlua
1 cup mini chocolate chip morsels

## Icing

1 cup heavy whipping cream
9 oz. semisweet chocolate morsels
2 Tbsp. Kahlua

## Directions

Preheat oven to 350 degrees. In a large bowl, add the cake mix and pudding mix and stir to blend. In another bowl, stir together the eggs, oil, coffee, and $^{2}/_{3}$ cup Kahlua until smooth. Gently fold wet ingredients into dry ingredients. Add the 1 cup mini chocolate chips. Transfer to a greased Bundt pan. Bake on lower middle rack for 45 minutes or until toothpick inserted in center comes out clean. Cool on wire rack.

Meanwhile, pour the heavy whipping cream into a pot and bring to a boil. Remove from heat. Stir in the 9 oz. semisweet chocolate morsels and 2 Tbsp. Kahlua until smooth. Drizzle over cake as a glaze. Slice and serve.

# LEMON BARS

*These lemon bars will seduce you into thinking they're light and airy and won't sabotage your weight. Substitute them for lemon meringue pie for an easy-to-grab sweet on the go.*

## Ingredients

Crust
$1/_2$ cup butter, softened
$1/_4$ cup sugar
1 cup flour

Filling
$1/_2$ cup sugar
2 eggs
3 Tbsp. lemon juice
2 Tbsp. flour
$1/_4$ tsp. baking powder
$1/_4$ tsp. freshly grated nutmeg

Topping
1 Tbsp. powdered sugar

## Directions

Preheat oven to 350 degrees. In a small bowl, cream butter and sugar, then add flour in small batches until mixture is blended. Press into an ungreased 8-inch square baking dish. Bake for 15 to 20 minutes or until slightly browned. Meanwhile, in a separate bowl, beat the filling ingredients until frothy. Pour over crust. Bake for 10 to 15 minutes or until set. Cool on a wire rack. Sprinkle with powdered sugar and cut into squares to serve. Makes 12 to 16 lemon bars.

Nancy J. Cohen

# LEMON BREAD PUDDING

*My grandmother made this recipe for one of our visits. I don't remember much about her, but when she died, my mother was especially grateful to find her stash of hand-written recipes. I really like the unique lemony flavor of this bread pudding along with the golden raisins. Add the sauce, and it's a lip-smacking after-dinner treat. If you don't eat bread puddings often, at least try this one.*

**Ingredients**

Pudding
2 cups dry bread cubes
4 cups scalded milk
1 Tbsp. unsalted butter, softened
$1/4$ tsp. salt
$3/4$ cup sugar
4 eggs, slightly beaten
1 tsp. vanilla
$1/2$ cup golden raisins

Sauce
$1/2$ cup sugar
1 Tbsp. cornstarch
$1/8$ tsp. salt
$1/8$ tsp. freshly grated nutmeg
1 cup boiling water
2 Tbsp. unsalted butter, softened
$1^1/2$ Tbsp. fresh lemon juice

## Directions

Preheat oven to 350 degrees. Soak bread in hot milk for 5 minutes. Add 1 Tbsp. butter, ¼ tsp. salt, and ¾ cup sugar and stir to blend. Pour eggs over while stirring. Add vanilla and raisins; stir to combine. Pour mixture into greased 9x13x2 inch glass baking dish. Place the baking dish into a pan of shallow hot water. The water should come halfway up the sides of the baking dish. Bake until set, about 50 minutes. When done, remove bread pudding dish from pan with water and cool on rack.

Meanwhile, mix $1/2$ cup sugar, cornstarch, $1/8$ tsp. salt and nutmeg for sauce in a medium saucepan. Gradually add boiling water and stir. Cook over low heat until thick and clear. Add butter and lemon juice. Whisk to blend. Pour over baked pudding. Chill dish in refrigerator until ready to serve.

# LYCHEE PINEAPPLE UPSIDE DOWN CAKE

*This tropical variation on an old favorite was my mother's creation. Try to get fresh lychees when you can because the sweetness will be more intense.*

## Ingredients

5 Tbsp. unsalted butter
$1/_2$ cup brown sugar
8 oz. can pineapple slices in juice
10 oz. jar Maraschino cherries
1 cup fresh lychees or 1 can lychees, drained and chopped
15.25 oz. box classic vanilla cake mix
3 eggs
$1/_3$ cup vegetable oil
$2/_3$ cup pineapple juice reserved from can
$1/_2$ cup water

## Directions

Preheat oven to 350 degrees. Melt butter in microwave. Pour melted butter into greased 9x13x2 inch baking pan. Sprinkle brown sugar on top. Drain pineapple slices, reserving liquid. Arrange pineapple slices in single layer on top of brown sugar mixture. Add cherries in center of each slice and sprinkle around a few chopped lychees.

In a large bowl, combine cake mix, eggs, oil, reserved pineapple juice, and water. Whisk mixture for 2 minutes. Pour half of the cake batter on top of the pineapple, cherries and lychees. Chop remaining pineapple rings and then spread over the batter, together with remaining lychees. Pour rest of cake batter on top of the second fruit layer.

Bake for 50 minutes or until cake is set and a toothpick inserted in center comes out clean. Remove from oven, cover loosely with foil, and let stand for 10 minutes. Chill in the refrigerator for at least an hour. Slice and serve.

# LYCHEE RICE PUDDING

*If you're fond of rice pudding, you'll like this recipe with fresh lychees for added zing. The exotic fruit will liven up this classic dessert.*

## Ingredients

2 medium bananas, sliced
2 cups fresh lychees, chopped
$1/_2$ cup water
4 Tbsp. honey
2 tsp. vanilla
1 tsp. ground cinnamon
1 tsp. freshly ground nutmeg
3 cups cooked brown rice
2 cups nonfat milk

## Directions

In a medium-size saucepan, combine bananas, lychees, water, honey, vanilla, cinnamon and nutmeg. Bring to a boil, reduce the heat, and simmer for 10 minutes, or until tender but not mushy. Add the rice and milk and mix thoroughly. Top with a sprinkle of freshly grated nutmeg at serving time. Serves 4.

# ORANGE COINTREAU CAKE

*This recipe is a good way to use some of the liqueur sitting in your cabinet. If desired, serve warm with whipped topping.*

## Ingredients

2 cups all-purpose flour
1 cup sugar
$1/_2$ cup unsalted butter, room temperature
2 tsp. cinnamon
2 tsp. baking powder
Dash salt
2 eggs
$3/_4$ cup orange juice
$1/_4$ cup Cointreau
1 tsp. orange zest

## Directions

Preheat oven to 350 degrees. Combine flour, sugar, and softened butter until mixture resembles crumbs. Remove 1 cup of mixture and add cinnamon. Set this portion aside for topping. Add baking powder and a dash of salt to the first bowl.

In a separate bowl, beat eggs by fork with orange juice and Cointreau. Stir liquid into the flour mixture and add orange zest. Mix until blended.

Pour batter into a greased and floured 9x13x2 inch baking pan. Sprinkle reserved topping over the cake batter. Bake for 30 minutes, or until a toothpick inserted in center comes out clean. Cut into squares and serve warm.

# PEAR BLUEBERRY COFFEE CAKE

*Mixing pears with blueberries gives you a double whammy in terms of getting your fruit portions for the day. And using a prepared mix cuts down on prep time, which makes this one a snap. It's a great recipe for a brunch. If you cannot obtain the blueberry bread mix, another fruit flavor would work as well.*

## Ingredients

16.9 oz. box blueberry quick bread mix
$^3/_4$ cup water
$^1/_4$ cup vegetable oil
2 eggs
15 oz. can pears, drained and thinly sliced
1 tsp. lemon juice
$^1/_3$ cup flour
$^1/_3$ cup sugar
$^1/_2$ tsp. ground cinnamon
2 Tbsp. unsalted butter, melted

## Directions

Preheat oven to 375 degrees. Prepare the bread mix batter with water, vegetable oil, and eggs according to package directions. Pour into a greased 9-inch square baking dish. In a separate bowl, sprinkle pear slices with lemon juice. Arrange pear slices over batter.

In another small bowl, combine the flour, sugar, and cinnamon, then add melted butter and stir. Mixture will be crumbly. Sprinkle over pears. Bake for 40 minutes or until toothpick inserted in center comes out clean. Cool on rack. Slice and serve.

# PEAR CAKE

*Molasses is one ingredient I never tire of using. This pear cake is lip-smacking delicious especially when served warm with vanilla ice cream.*

## Ingredients

6 Tbsp. unsalted butter, divided
$1/4$ cup firmly packed dark brown sugar
2 large cans sliced pears in light syrup, drained
$11/4$ cups all purpose flour
$3/4$ tsp. baking powder
$3/4$ tsp. baking soda
$1/4$ tsp. salt
$1/2$ tsp. ground cinnamon
$1/4$ tsp. ground ginger
$1/2$ tsp. ground nutmeg
$1/4$ tsp. ground coriander
$1/2$ cup sugar
1 large egg
$1/3$ cup buttermilk
$1/2$ tsp. pure vanilla extract
2 Tbsp. unsulphured molasses

## Directions

Preheat oven to 350 degrees. Melt 2 Tbsp. butter and spread on bottom of 9x13x2 inch baking pan. Sprinkle brown sugar over melted butter. Arrange pear slices over brown sugar. Meanwhile, combine flour, baking powder, baking soda, salt and spices in a medium bowl.

In a large bowl, cream remaining 4 Tbsp. softened butter with $1/2$ cup sugar until smooth. Blend in 1 egg, buttermilk, vanilla and molasses. Add dry ingredients slowly and stir until mixed through. Spread batter evenly over pears.

Bake for 20 to 30 minutes, or until a toothpick inserted in center comes out clean. Cool on rack. Invert onto plate. Slice and serve warm.

# PUMPKIN MOUSSE

*This recipe popped out at me in a Thanksgiving issue of a popular food magazine. I took a photo with my cell phone, copied it onto my computer at home, and adjusted the ingredients for my taste. It's frothy and light and the perfect finale for a holiday meal.*

## Ingredients

1$^1/_2$ cups fat free milk
1 oz. package sugar free instant butterscotch pudding mix
$^1/_2$ cup canned pumpkin
$^1/_2$ tsp. ground cinnamon
$^1/_4$ tsp. ground ginger
$^1/_4$ tsp. ground allspice
$^1/_2$ cup fat free whipped topping
$^1/_4$ tsp. freshly grated nutmeg

## Directions

Whisk milk and pudding mix in large bowl for two minutes. Set aside. In another bowl, combine the pumpkin, cinnamon, ginger, and allspice. Add to the pudding mixture. Gently fold in whipped topping until blended. Spoon into individual dessert cups. Sprinkle nutmeg on top. Refrigerate until ready to serve. Serves 4 to 6.

# SPICED PEACH CAKE

*This is so easy to make that it's a whiz to prepare. Serve for brunch or after dinner with a scoop of vanilla ice cream. Or bring it to a dessert party and impress your friends.*

## Ingredients

15.25 oz. box spice cake mix
$1/4$ tsp. cinnamon
1 cup buttermilk
$1/3$ cup vegetable oil
$1/3$ cup unsweetened applesauce
3 large eggs
21 oz. can peach pie filling

## Directions

Preheat oven to 350 degrees. Grease and flour a 9x13x2 inch baking pan. Mix together the cake mix, cinnamon, buttermilk, oil, applesauce and eggs in a large bowl. Beat on slow for one minute then increase speed for two more minutes. Pour batter into greased pan. Spoon peaches and syrup from the can evenly over the batter. Bake for 30 minutes or until toothpick inserted in center comes out clean. Slice and serve warm, if desired, with whipped topping or vanilla ice cream.

# STRAWBERRY COBBLER

*My friend Wendy supplied this recipe after she picked too many strawberries at Kinsdale Farms. It's a delicious way to share the pleasure and makes a tempting presentation.*

## Ingredients

32 oz. strawberries
$1/_2$ cup + 1 Tbsp. sugar
1 Tbsp. cornstarch
1 cup water
5 Tbsp. unsalted butter, diced
1 cup all-purpose flour
$1^1/_2$ tsp. baking powder
$1/_4$ tsp. cinnamon
$1/_2$ tsp. salt
$3/_4$ cup heavy whipping cream

## Directions

Preheat oven to 400 degrees. Hull, clean, and quarter the strawberries and set aside. Combine $1/_2$ cup sugar, cornstarch, and water in saucepan. Cook over medium heat, stirring constantly, until thickened. Stir in strawberries and remove from heat. Pour mixture into greased 9-inch square baking dish and dot with 2 Tbsp. diced butter.

In a large bowl, sift together the flour, 1 Tbsp. sugar, baking powder, cinnamon and salt. Cut in 3 Tbsp. diced butter. Stir in whipping cream. Mixture will be lumpy but somewhat soft. Drop by the teaspoonful on top of berries. Bake for 25 minutes or until golden brown and bubbly. Serves 6 to 8.

Nancy J. Cohen

# WINE CAKE

*My sister-in-law Charlene found this recipe when she and my brother toured the Napa Valley. It's a moist cake flavored by wine and easy to prepare.*

## Ingredients

15.25 oz. box yellow cake mix
3.4 oz. box vanilla instant pudding mix
6 eggs
$3/4$ cup oil
1 cup sweet white wine
1 tsp. freshly grated nutmeg
Powdered sugar

## Directions

Preheat oven to 350 degrees. Mix all ingredients in a large bowl. Beat with electric mixer for 5 minutes at medium speed. Pour batter into greased tube cake pan. Bake for 1 hour or until toothpick comes out clean. Cool on rack. Invert onto serving plate. Dust with powdered sugar, or mix powdered sugar with enough milk to moisten and dribble glaze over cake. Slice and serve.

# TRIMMED TO DEATH

## Bad Hair Day Mystery #15

**The Recipes**
Apple Rum Cake
Chicken Cacciatore
Chicken Tenderloins
Chocolate Kahlua Cake
Coconut Fudge Pie
Eggplant Rollatini
Lemon Bread Pudding
Mushroom Pie
Peach Cobbler
Vegetable Gumbo

**The Story**
Savvy hairstylist and amateur sleuth Marla Vail enters a charity bake-off contest at a fall festival sponsored by a local farm. While she waits to see if her coconut fudge pie is a winner, Marla joins a scavenger hunt where people playing character roles are the targets. Instead of scoring points with a live person, she finds a dead body planted face-down in the strawberry field. Who would want to cut short the life of food magazine publisher and fellow bake-off contestant, Francine Dodger? As she investigates, Marla learns there's no shortage of suspects. A celebrity TV chef, food critic, olive oil importer, food truck owner, pastry chef, and cookbook author may be stirring up more than their next recipe. Can Marla unmask the killer before someone else gets trimmed from life?

## Excerpt from Trimmed to Death

"Here they come. Look sharp," Marla Vail said to her friend, Tally Riggs. The judges headed down the line in their direction. Marla's heart rate accelerated as they got closer. Being the last two contestants might be a good thing. Tally and Marla's entries would linger in the judges' minds more so than the other ten, even if those included chocolate Kahlua cake, blueberry crumble, and plum almond tarts.

"The money raised by the bake-off goes to a good cause," Tally reminded her. "It doesn't matter if we win or not." She stood next to Marla behind a table displaying her lemon bread pudding. Tally brushed a stray blond hair off her model-perfect face. Her tall frame made Marla's five-foot six-inch height feel short.

"I know, but a ten-thousand-dollar business grant is hard to let go." Marla wanted to add a bistro to her hair salon and day spa. Winning the prize would allow her to move forward with her plans. But she'd be happier if Tally won. Her widowed friend had yet to reopen her dress shop after the horrific car crash that had killed her husband and put her in the hospital. Despite having generous benefits from Ken's life insurance policy, Tally could use the money to raise her son and rebuild her business.

"Look at the crowd," Tally pointed out. "Ticket sales must be good."

People gathered by the cluster of tables under white tent awnings. From the paper plates and plastic forks in their hands, they couldn't wait for the judging to end so they could sample the goods. As instructed, both Marla and Tally had brought extra portions.

A strong breeze swept by, lifting the corners of their tablecloths. An early October cold front in South Florida made Marla glad she'd worn a sweater along with jeans and ankle boots. Dry grass crunched underfoot as she shifted her feet. The day had turned out sunny with clear skies for the fall harvest festival at Kinsdale Farms. Located at the western edge of Broward County, the produce farm hosted this event each year. Various businesses sponsored the competitions that entrants applied for months in advance.

One of the judges lingered at table number eight to speak to the caramel-skinned woman there. He must have said something that displeased her, because her mouth thinned and her eyes narrowed. Marla recognized the judge as Carlton Paige, food critic. His pudgy face and rotund figure were hard to miss. Rumor said restaurateurs cringed when he entered their premises. The lady's response made his lips curl in a sneer before he moved on.

Now only two entrants separated the judges from Marla. She glanced at the women but they were strangers to her. She'd been busy setting up earlier and hadn't met the other contenders, although Teri DuMond was a familiar face. The chocolatier ran tours at the factory where she sold artisan chocolates. Teri had waved a greeting to Marla before the judging began.

Marla's breath came short as the judges neared. It was silly to feel so nervous. Nonetheless, she scanned the throng looking for her husband Dalton's reassuring figure but spied him nowhere. He had entered his own competition for best homegrown tomatoes. That contest awarded a hundred-dollar gift certificate to a plant nursery.

"Number eleven, what is it you have for us?" said the sole female judge in a Southern accent. Marla's attention whipped forward. The judge wore her bleached hair piled high atop her head like cotton candy. Her rosy lips formed a pout as she regarded Marla with an assessing glance. Huge gold hoop earrings matched the heavy chains around her neck.

"My entry is a coconut fudge pie. You must be Raquel Hayes. I watch your cooking show on TV. It's an honor to meet you. All of you," Marla amended hastily.

Tristan Marsh looked down his nose at her. The pastry chef from The Royal Palate made up the last of their trio. He had a thin face with a pasty complexion like the flour he used in his confections. From his slender frame, she surmised he had a fast metabolism, spent a lot of time at the gym, or didn't taste too many of his own creations.

Carlton Paige, the food critic, picked up a plastic fork and a sample slice of her dish. "God, I hope this isn't as awful as the last few entries. They tasted like cardboard," he said in an annoying nasal tone.

Raquel grimaced. "I've had my fill of sweets for the day. This one had better be good."

"None of them can equal my artistry," Tristan announced. He put a piece in his mouth and rolled it around on his tongue before he chewed and swallowed. His face gave nothing away about his opinion.

"Oh, come on, you can't expect these amateurs to do anything fancy," Carlton replied. His brows lifted as he tasted her dessert. Marla took that as a hopeful sign.

"Marla might not be in the food industry, but she's a great baker," Tally said in Marla's defense. "She used to experiment with rare fruit recipes. You'd love her lychee upside-down cake. I told her she had to enter this contest."

Marla's cheeks warmed. "Tally likes anything with chocolate. She doesn't have to worry about her figure like I do. If I didn't love her, I'd be envious."

Carlton gave Tally a smarmy onceover. "You're not too thin, which is a good thing. A man likes a good handful, if you know what I mean."

"Keep it in your pants, lover boy," Tristan admonished him. He glanced at Raquel, who'd tasted Marla's entry. "Well, how do you like it?" The pastry chef's effeminate gesture matched his manner of speech.

"You know I can't talk in front of the contestants. You'll see after the tallies are done. Tally, you get it?" Raquel flicked a glance at Marla's friend and chuckled at her pun. Her breasts jiggled with her movements.

*Dear Lord, this trio of clowns is judging our entries?* They seemed less than thrilled to be there. The publicity must be worth it. All of them would benefit from being in the spotlight.

"I don't have a hope in hell of winning," said the lady on Marla's left after the judges departed. All the winners from the various contests would be announced later. "I'm Alyce Greene, by the way."

Marla admired the woman's white bomber jacket with silver trim decorating each sleeve. "I'm Marla Vail, and this is my friend, Tally Riggs. It's our first time doing a bake-off contest."

"I'm glad to see so many guests. Ticket sales must be brisk. That'll be great for the Safety First Alliance."

The non-profit organization educated the public against leaving children and pets in hot cars. Marla had signed up as a volunteer when she'd heard about their cause. "Yes, I understand eighty percent of the proceeds will be donated to the group," she said. "I wish it could be more, but I suppose the sponsoring company has to make back some of their administrative costs."

The contestants handed out dessert samples to the crowd that converged on their booths. The guests had each paid a dollar per ticket, which entitled them to one item. Some gluttons descended on the tables with handfuls of tickets.

"What would you two do with the prize money if you win?" Alyce asked Marla and Tally once the mob dispersed.

Each contestant had paid a fifty-dollar entry fee along with the submission of a business plan that included a food component. City council members had vetted the proposals and selected the entrants. Marla felt lucky to be chosen, although she'd entered more due to Tally's urging than a desire to win.

285

"I own a salon and day spa," she replied. "If I had the extra cash, I'd add a bistro menu to my services."

"And I plan to open a boutique café," Tally commented. "It's a hot concept, combining a clothing store with food services. How about you?"

Alyce gave them a wry glance. "I don't need the funds for myself. I write a popular food blog, and it's monetized through affiliate ads. My husband owns a food truck operation. I'd pay off his starter loan so he could expand the business."

"What's this I heard about funds?" The contestant on Alyce's other side wandered in their direction.

Alyce frowned at her. "I was just telling them about my food blog. Ladies, have you met Francine Dodger?"

Marla and Tally introduced themselves, while Marla noted similarities between the other two women. Both had brown hair and similar statures. Alyce's eyes matched her brunette hair color, while Francine had green eyes, but otherwise they shared the same even features.

"I love your hairstyles," Marla said. "Those pixie cuts look cute on both of you. Where do you get your hair done?"

"We go to the same stylist. It's Karen at Salon Style," Alyce replied.

"Are you related to each other?"

Francine darted a glance at Alyce before responding. "If we were, I'd convince Alyce to blog for my publication. I'm the publisher of *Eat Well Now* magazine." She shivered in the cool air and wrapped her arms around her chest.

Without a sweater, Francine must be cold in her short-sleeved top. Its purple color along with her green eyes reminded Marla of Mardi Gras in New Orleans.

"I'm a subscriber," Tally said in an eager tone. "I love the Vintage Finds column. That's my favorite section."

Marla had heard of the periodical but hadn't read it. "I like to cook, but my passion is doing hair. My reading tastes lean toward trade journals and hair fashion magazines."

"What's the name of your salon?" Alyce asked.

"It's the Cut 'N Dye. May I give you my card?"

The other women reached into their purses, and they all exchanged business cards.

"You must be freezing in that skimpy top," Alyce said to Francine. She took off her white bomber jacket. "Here, wear this. You'll need it to stay warm during the game, but don't get it dirty or you'll pay for the cleaning bill."

"Thanks, it's colder than I'd expected today." Francine accepted the jacket and threw it on. "Are you ladies joining the live scavenger hunt?"

Tally gaped at her. "Don't tell me you're Find Franny?"

Francine's mouth split into a grin. "Yep, that's me. The game is so much fun each year, and Kinsdale Farms has so many places to hide."

Marla glanced at her watch. They had to load their supplies into the car before participating in other activities.

"We'd better get this stuff cleaned up," she said. "The kids' craft corner starts in twenty minutes, and I see the organizers eyeing our tables."

Alyce and Francine left to clear their spots, while Marla retrieved a large trash bag from her stash of supplies.

"Let's meet back at the ticket booth," Tally suggested, stacking the empty paper plates on her table. "We have some free time before the Find Franny game starts."

"Okay, but I'd like to meet the other contestants before we leave."

**ORDER NOW** at
https://nancyjcohen.com/trimmed-to-death/

# Themed Menus

It's always fun when you have a themed dinner party. Some of these recipes you can find in these pages. Others are suggestions for dishes you can look up on your own. Or substitute your choices instead. At any rate, I hope these ideas will inspire you to be creative in the kitchen.

**Caribbean Night**
Guacamole with Corn Chips
Pumpkin Chicken Soup
Coconut Shrimp
Island Turkey Thighs
Caribbean Rice with Pigeon Peas
Apple Rum Cake

**French Night**
French Onion Soup
Chicken Divine
Potatoes Au Gratin
Green Beans Almondine
Chocolate Eclairs

**Greek Night**
Olive Medley
Tzatziki Dip with Pita Bread
Spanakopita
Greek Salad
Moussaka
Grilled Lamb Skewers
Baklava

**Italian Night**
Caesar Salad
Garlic Bread
Eggplant Parmesan
Turkey Tetrazzini
Spaghetti
Steamed Broccoli
Tiramisu

**Latin Night**
Black Bean Soup
Pan-Fried Tilapia
Ropa Vieja
Spanish Rice
Fried Sweet Plantains
Yucca Casserole
Caramel Flan

**Asian Night**
Baked Egg Rolls
Wonton Soup
Chicken Teriyaki
Fried Rice
Stir-Fried Vegetables
Lychee Pineapple Upside Down Cake

# Holiday Dinners

**Easter**
Deviled Eggs
Spinach Salad
Roast Leg of Lamb
Rosemary Red Potatoes
Fresh Asparagus
Carrot Cake

**Passover**
Haroset
Hard Boiled Eggs with Salt Water Dip
Gefilte Fish
Chicken Soup with Matzo Balls
Brisket with Dried Plums
Tzimmes (sweet potatoes and prunes from Brisket recipe)
Macaroons

**Rosh Hashanah**
Apple Slices & Honey
Gefilte Fish
Chicken Soup with Matzo Balls
Brisket Cola
Noodle Kugel
Roasted Acorn Squash
Honey Cake

**Thanksgiving**
Cranberry Bread
Butternut Squash Soup
Roast Turkey with Cranberry Sauce
Sweet Potatoes with Marshmallows
Green Bean Casserole
Pumpkin Pie

Nancy J. Cohen

**Hanukkah**
Chopped Liver with Crackers
Eggplant Dip
Brisket with Cranberries and Molasses
Potato Latkes with Applesauce or Sour Cream
Broccoli Cheese Bake
Hanukkah Cookies

**Christmas**
Wassail
Christmas Ham or Roast Turkey Breast
Sweet Potato Casserole
Mashed Potatoes
Roasted Cauliflower
Chocolate Yule Log

# Books with Recipes

## The Bad Hair Day Mysteries

### Easter Hair Hunt (Book 16)
Garlic Cheese Biscuits
Slow Cooker Roast Leg of Lamb
Slow Cooker Mushroom Pot Roast
Roasted Acorn Squash
Rosemary Red Potatoes
Tilapia Dijon

### Trimmed to Death (Book 15)
Chicken Cacciatore
Chicken Tenderloins
Eggplant Rollatini
Mushroom Pie
Vegetable Gumbo
Apple Rum Cake
Chocolate Kahlua Cake
Coconut Fudge Pie
Lemon Bread Pudding
Peach Cobbler

### Hairball Hijinks (Short Story)
Chicken Orzo
Eggplant Tomato Casserole
Roasted Red Potatoes
Shrimp Brown Rice
Chocolate Zucchini Cake

Nancy J. Cohen

**Hanging by a Hair (Book 11)**
Brisket with Dried Plums
Chicken Spaghetti
Israeli Couscous with Mushrooms
Pot Roast
Salmon Croquettes

**Killer Knots (Book 9)**
Island Turkey Thighs
Caribbean Rice with Pigeon Peas
Apple Ginger Cake

**Highlights to Heaven (Book 5)**
Haroset for Passover

# A Sabbath Dinner

## By Minnie Heller

*Note from Nancy: This special article was written by my mother. Enjoy this peek into my family history in a bygone era. This celebrates the Sabbath and the special dinner for this day of rest.*

Our Sabbath, to which we as a family all looked forward, began on the Thursday before Saturday. We were awakened by the tantalizing fragrance of fresh baked braided challahs and onion board, or *pletzels* as we called them. We devoured the onion board at breakfast. Mama had already done a half day's work by the time we awoke for school. We used to say that she went to bed with the chickens, which was right after dinner, and awoke with the chickens at 5 A.M.

By the time we got home from school, she had all her bread baked and the delicious yeast cakes filled with white raisins that we loved. She had a lot of baking to do for a family with eight children. Also the chicken, chosen from our flock, whose bottom had already been inspected not to be with eggs, had been slaughtered by the *shoichet* down the street.

When I was home on a Thursday, Mama sent me with the chicken to the *shoichet*. It was a painful experience for me each time I had to go—to see the *shoichet* pluck a few feathers from the throat of the chicken, slit its throat and then hang the chicken upside down on a stick balanced over a barrel, with the chicken's feet tied together, until the blood stopped oozing into the barrel.

When the chicken was determined to be dead, it was wrapped in newspaper and taken home. Mama proceeded to pluck or flick the chicken, and then to eviscerate it and prepare it to go into the pot.

Next she mixed her dough for noodles, rolled it out until it was paper thin, then rolled the thin layer into a sausage and proceeded to cut it into very thin strips with such speed that I marveled she didn't cut her fingers off in the process. Now came the time to concentrate on the fish for the Sabbath. This chore she delegated to me.

With instructions and coins in my pocket, I headed for Mr. Bloomfield's houseboat on a creek that was a tributary of the Platte River, which ran north and south in Colorado. Mr. Bloomfield was always dressed in large rubber boots and wore a big apron. He had several trap doors on the floor of his large room on this houseboat. I would tell him how many pounds the carp should weigh, on which Mama instructed me. He would lift the trap door of the many fish weighing each that much, put in his long-handled net, and catch the fish I requested.

After I paid for it, he wrapped it in newspapers. I put it under my arm and away I went, with the fish wiggling to escape. As soon as I got home, the fish went into the bathtub, which had been filled with water, to stay there until the next morning at 6 A.M.

On Friday, we were awakened by the sound of chopping of the fish that Mama had already cleaned. She added all the necessary ingredients for gefilte fish, and then wrapped the fish mixture in the skin she had cut away. The aroma of gefilte fish cooking in hot juices is a nostalgic memory I will never forget.

Next Mama cooked her chicken and soup, the noodles, and lastly, a fruit compote. When her cooking was done, she scrubbed our large kitchen floor with its inlaid linoleum.

By this time, we had come home from school, and we took turns getting bathed. We had a bath once a week on Fridays. We then put on clean clothes. After Mama put a white tablecloth on the table, a five-candlestick silver candelabra, two covered challahs, wine in a large Kiddush cup, and salt, we were ready to greet the bride—Sabbath.

Papa went to shule at sundown with my brothers. Mama was too tired to go on Friday night. Wearing a *sheitel*, or a wig, so she did not have to cover her head, she lit the five candles. She covered her eyes while she blessed the candles, and asked God to bless our home, the children, all the family, and our friends. We anxiously awaited the arrival of Papa and the boys. When he got home, Papa exchanged his hat for a yarmulke and also gave a yarmulke to each boy.

After we were seated around the beautiful table, Papa made Kiddush, sipped from the glass of wine, then passed it around for each one of us to take a sip. Then he made *hamotzi* over the freshly baked bread, cut off the corner, sprinkled it with salt, tasted it, cut more slices, and passed it around. We each did the same thing. The Friday night meal followed, ending with compote for dessert.

Afterwards, Papa and the boys sang Sabbath songs until it was time to go to bed. Before bedtime, Fred, a black man, arrived to stoke the fire in the coal stove. He added enough coal and kindling to last all night. He then turned out the light. In the morning, before we got up, he came again, cleaned out the ashes and put more coal on to last all day.

Saturday morning, we were again awakened by tantalizing aromas of the *cholent* or stew baking in the oven overnight. After breakfast (Papa didn't eat), Papa left with the boys to his shule, located about ten blocks away on the other side of the Platte River. It was a Chassidic shule. Mama and the girls went to a shule located much closer on Dale Court in Denver. The women sat upstairs and were separated by a curtain from the men who prayed downstairs. We children played outdoors until the services were over.

The boys did not fare so well. They had to stay right near Papa and participate in the services as much as they knew how. We went home with Mama, Papa coming much later because of the distance. Occasionally, Papa brought home a guest from the shule, a stranger passing by the town, or a newcomer seeking friends, to share our meal. It was Maimonides, in his Laws of Festivals, who wrote that a Sabbath table with the presence of an orphan, widow or unfortunate, expresses the rejoicing of the festival instead of the rejoicing of the stomach. We then had dinner in much the same manner as the night before.

Papa napped in the afternoon while Mama visited with friends and neighbors in our home, serving her delicious yeast cakes and glasses of tea. I was always fascinated to see our guests use sugar lumps that they placed on their tongues, sipping the tea by sucking it through the cube of sugar. I often wondered why they did not choke on the cube.

While these guests were entertained, we children played or read. We were not allowed to write or ride on the Sabbath. Often we walked to the park and enjoyed the beauty of the foliage.

After Papa's nap, he went to the Rabbi's house, about four blocks away. With about eleven other disciples, he sat around a long refectory table and listened to the wise and brilliant discourse of our Rabbi, who sat at the head of the table propounding the difficult interpretations of the Talmud and the Torah.

Just before Sundown, Papa went again to shule for *Mincha* and *Maariv* services. After the first star was visible in the heavens as a sign that the Sabbath was at an end, the *Havdalah* service was performed to say Goodbye to the Sabbath and Hello to the weekdays.

Papa came home after dark. He handed me a beautiful braided candle with red, white and blue colors. It was a tall candle. Then he made Kiddush in a silver Kiddush glass and drank the wine. He took a spice container and passed it around for all of us to smell the fragrance of the sweet herbs. He lit the candle of many strands and recited the blessing, lifting up his hands to look at the light through his fingers.

At the end of the blessing, he doused the candle into the cup of remaining wine. We children then dipped our pinky fingers into the blessed wine and wiped them in our pockets (we made sure we all had pockets) so that our future years would bring not only health, but wealth too. So ended our beautiful Sabbath, with the greeting of *Shavua Tov*, Have a good week!

Nancy J. Cohen

# Acknowledgments

I offer my deep gratitude to the following readers who offered invaluable suggestions, insightful comments, and proofreading for this book. I couldn't have completed this project without their helpful critique, sharp reading skills, and expertise. In alphabetical order:

Ana M. Kurland
Jan Perrone
Kitty Philips, Private Chef and Culinary Instructor
Patty Rosellini
Rhonda Gilliland, Author and Editor of the Cooked to Death Series
Taryn Lee

Again, my sincere thanks go to these dedicated readers who gave their time to help me improve this book.

## Author's Note

I learned how to cook from the best teacher—my mother. Fond memories show her in the kitchen while I did my homework at the kitchen table. I love to cook and experiment with recipes. I've taken cooking classes, read cooking magazines, and collected enough cookbooks to fill several bookshelves. It's fun to try new dishes. Most of the time, they turn out okay. Sometimes, they don't, and that's part of the learning process. These pages include my favorite recipes. I hope you'll enjoy making them.

If you like this cookbook, please write a review at your favorite online bookstore. Customer reviews are extremely important in attracting new readers to my work.

For updates on my new releases, giveaways, special offers and events, join my reader list at https://nancyjcohen.com/newsletter. Free Book Sampler for new subscribers.

## About the Author

Nancy J. Cohen writes The Bad Hair Day Mysteries featuring South Florida hairstylist Marla Vail. Titles in this series have been named Best Cozy Mystery by *Suspense Magazine*, won a Readers' Favorite gold medal, earned first place in the Chanticleer International Book Awards and third place in the Arizona Literary Awards, and made the finals in the American Fiction Awards. Nancy's instructional guide, *Writing the Cozy Mystery*, was nominated for an Agatha Award and won a gold medal in the President's Book Awards from Florida Authors and Publishers Association.

A featured speaker at libraries, conferences, and community events, Nancy is listed in *Contemporary Authors, Poets & Writers*, and *Who's Who in U.S. Writers, Editors, & Poets.* When not busy writing, she enjoys cooking, fine dining, cruising, visiting Disney World, and shopping. Contact her at nancy@nancyjcohen.com

### Follow Nancy Online

Website - https://nancyjcohen.com
Blog - https://nancyjcohen.com/blog
Twitter - https://www.twitter.com/nancyjcohen
Facebook - https://www.facebook.com/NancyJCohenAuthor
Goodreads - https://www.goodreads.com/nancyjcohen
Pinterest - https://pinterest.com/njcohen/
LinkedIn - https://www.linkedin.com/in/nancyjcohen
Instagram - https://instagram.com/nancyjcohen
BookBub - https://www.bookbub.com/authors/nancy-j-cohen
Booklover's Bench - https://bookloversbench.com

# Books by Nancy J. Cohen

*Bad Hair Day Mysteries*
Permed to Death
Hair Raiser
Murder by Manicure
Body Wave
Highlights to Heaven
Died Blonde
Dead Roots
Perish by Pedicure
Killer Knots
Shear Murder
Hanging by a Hair
Peril by Ponytail
Haunted Hair Nights (Novella)
Facials Can Be Fatal
Hair Brained
Hairball Hijinks (Short Story)
Trimmed to Death
Easter Hair Hunt

*Anthology*
"Three Men and a Body" in Wicked Women Whodunit

*The Drift Lords Series*
Warrior Prince
Warrior Rogue
Warrior Lord

*Science Fiction Romances*
Keeper of the Rings
Silver Serenade

Nancy J. Cohen

***The Light-Years Series***
Circle of Light
Moonlight Rhapsody
Starlight Child

***Nonfiction***
Writing the Cozy Mystery
A Bad Hair Day Cookbook

**For more details, go to** http://nancyjcohen.com/books/

CPSIA information can be obtained
at www.ICGtesting.com
Printed in the USA
LVHW011730081119
636788LV00008B/560